GOD'S GRACE,
CHILI DOGS,
& SUPPER AT
MAMA'S

Traditional Southern
Appalachian Cooking

Richard Pruett '1994

RICHARD H. PARROTT

GOD'S GRACE, CHILI DOGS & SUPPER AT MAMA'S

Traditional Southern Appalachian Cooking

Parnassus Publishing
Morristown, Tennessee

Parnassus Publishing; P. O. Box 14202; Manley Station; Morristown, TN 37814

Scripture taken from the HOLY BIBLE, NEW INTERNATIONAL VERSION Copyright 1973, 1978, 1984 International Bible Society. Used by permission of Zondervan Bible Publishers.

Library of Congress Catalog Card Number: 93-87637

Publisher's Cataloging in Publication
(Prepared by Quality Books Inc.)

Parrott, Richard H.
    God's grace, chili dogs & supper at Mama's: traditional Southern Appalachian cooking / Richard H. Parrott.
    p. cm.
    Includes index.
    ISBN 0-9639878-8-7
    1. Cookery, American--Southern style. 2. Cookery--Appalachian Region, Southern. 3. Appalachian Region, Southern--Social life and customs. I. Title. II. Title: God's grace, chili dogs and supper at Mama's.

TX715.S68P37 1994   641.5'975
                                      QBI93-22670

Printed in the United States of America
FIRST EDITION

Dedication

*This book is first
and lovingly dedicated to Jesus of Nazareth,
the living Son of God,
in hope that He finds it a pleasing endeavor;
to Mama, Gerry Parrott Asher, for her recipes and all the
excellent food she has prepared
over the years;
to my beautiful girls,
Pat and Beth for their love, help and patience;
to sister Joy Rutledge for being a joy;
to Christian;
to another Mama, Elsie Sparks;
to Dr. Daniel Green of U.T. Hospital in Knoxville,
Dr. Emmett Manley of Jefferson City,
Dr. Doug Evans of MD Anderson Cancer Clinic in
Houston,
Dr. Rick Fogle of U.T. Hospital in Knoxville, and
Dr. Tracy Dobbs, all
instruments of God's Grace;
to Mike Hodges of Manley Baptist Church, for his valuable
assistance and encouragement;
and to the memory of two fathers,
George P. Sparks, and
Hubert "Trap" Parrott and his friend
Isaiah.*

The Golden Sun

THE MEADOW IS QUIET.
The fog settles with a
hush soft as compassion, waiting
the burning wash of
golden green sunlight.

Near the mulberry tree,
close to a rock (hidden
by the tall grass passed
when the man mows the hay)
the borrow of the fox
lies concealed, secret.

The mother lies curled around
two pups, comforted by their
warmth.

One moves.
She touches with her nose;
warm, tart-sweet scent,
feels the coarseness of
it's fur.

The pup quiets
and the mother closes
her eyes, waiting the wash of
golden sun.

In a close thicket
deep inside a cedar; heavy, green
and concealing, a mockingbird
hides,

Feathers fluffed against the
wet cold, sleeping, dreaming of
the yellow Tom who comes

each morning from under
the farmer's house, to lie in the
golden sun.

The fog changes
from vapor to mist, wetting the
meadow and cedar, searching
escape from the
lightening horizon.

Inside the house
the only sound is the
tick of the warming window
panes.

A screen door slams
in the silence as the
sky brightens over the apple
trees alongside the meadow.

The yellow cat stirs
at the sound of the man's
footsteps on the porch.

A beam of sunlight
reflecting meadow green
strikes a window pane,
saturating the lace curtain
and makes a dappled pattern
on the crib.

The baby stirs,
raises her head and smiles at
the golden sun.

R. Parrott, 12-20-78
For Beth

Introduction

LET'S HAVE A CUP *of coffee and talk* . . . that's the flavor of this book. You see, it is more than just wonderful recipes that will send you to the kitchen for some down home cookin'. This book will bring back memories of your own as Rick shares with you his faith, his family and the food he grew up enjoying.

As I read through the first drafts I remembered a couple of daily rituals concerning food as I was growing up in Oklahoma. Every morning I was awakened by the smell of breakfast cooking and coffee brewing as Mother got Dad off to work. When I finally got out of bed and wandered into the living room, I would always see a nearly empty coffee cup and an open Bible at Mother's chair. You know, I take great comfort in recalling that Mother began her day with the Lord, His Word, and praying for her family.

My second recollection is Dad's words, "Our most gracious heavenly Father . . ." I was fortunate to have a God-loving father who insisted that we have at least one meal a day together as a family. Every evening when Mother called us to the table, we would bow our heads and Dad would begin to pray. What a remembrance . . . what an example to me!

See what I mean? Wonderful, warm times will return to your mind as you read Rick's own experiences. Soon you will not only be sharing recipes with someone; you will be swapping childhood memories!

Jesus said in Matthew 4:4, ". . . *man does not live on bread alone, but on every word that comes from the mouth of God.*" I hope you discover in this book a renewed fellowship with the Lord as you find not only cooking instruction, but also words for living in the scriptures and testimonies sprinkled throughout.

Paul said in 1 Corinthians 10:31, *"So whether you eat or drink or whatever you do, do it all for the glory of God."* I trust you will enjoy many times of wonderful fellowship around the table with your family, your friends, and with the Lord, partly because of this book. I know that will bring glory to God and in so doing, this book's author will feel that its purpose has been accomplished.

Rev. Mike Hodges, 1994

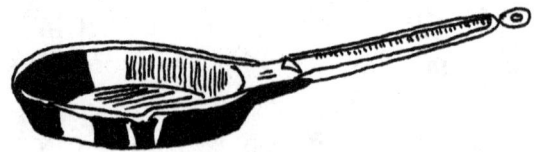

Preface

What good is it for a man to gain the whole world, and yet lose or forfeit his very self?   Luke 9:25

I grew up dreamin' of being a cowboy; and lovin' the cowboy ways; pursuing the lives of my high-riding heros, I burned up my childhood days; I learned all the rules of a modern-day drifter—don't ya hold on to nothin' too long . . .   S. Vaughan, performed by Willie Nelson

THE MOST FREQUENT COMMENT I hear when folks discover I am writing a book is, "how'd ya pick out sucha strange title? What's it mean, anyhow?" Well, it doesn't mean much, but it does mean something.

There was a mercenary motive behind the choice, also a logical one. The mercenary part is that a book title must grab attention. From the thousands and thousands of books published each year, the average book buyer sees only a small percentage. Of those, he probably gives little more than seven seconds to scanning the cover to decide if it is something he might be interested in purchasing. The title, then, must be something that will make him ask, "How'd he pick out sucha strange title?" God willing, he will flip through the book and just maybe see something there that will cause him to reach into his pocket.

Beyond that, I decided that if I were going to invest some part of my life into building a book, I wanted it to be something functional. A bit of market research told me that of Christian slanted publications, women make 80% of the purchases. Mama gave me sense enough to know that I had better write something that would appeal strongly to the female part of the household. "Okay," I thought, "what do I know about women?" Over the years I have come to realize that on a scale of one-ten I rate about minus two in my knowledge of and the understanding of women. Having a logical mind, though, my next question was, "what would Pat, my own adult female part of our household be inclined to buy?" I had the shrewdness to look in our bookcases. I discovered that of the volumes we own, Pat has bought (and these are the ones upstairs and not packed away in book hell, better know as the Parrott Basement) 208 cookbooks, and about seventy-three books concerning sewing and crafts. I'm serious—208 cookbooks!

My sole knowledge of the art of sewing is from my days of being single and discovering that if your pants need to be hemmed, and they are light in color, a SWINGLINE desk stapler does a nice job until about the fourth washing when the staples start to rust. I have, however, over the past forty-seven years, participated in the eating of some very good food. Cooking is fun if you have someone to clean up the mess (thank you Lord for Pat and Beth) so I personally enjoy cooking; and in my Mama's head are many recipes for a lot of good food. I chose cooking over sewing.

"Wait," I told myself, "a cookbook is okay, but what about the Great American Novel you promised yourself you would write someday?"

Somewhere inside my head, a voice said, "you can't dream of being a cowboy all your life."

"Yeah, I guess so," I answered, "but at least I can put something in it besides *recipes*." So you will find here some other stuff that came to my mind as I sat at the keyboard, the dog sleeping at my feet, looking out the window and typing.

I decided the "other stuff" had better be something our Lord would regard as worthy, or the time spent writing it would be about as valuable as a delicate spit in a high wind. *God's Grace* is the most important matter in any man's life. The Bible says it: (my paraphrase) "if you go through life and miss the grace of your Creator and His gift of Jesus as a Savior who reconciles you to God, then you have missed the whole point of existing." You *might as well* sing Cowboy songs to yourself all your life.

What about *Chili Dogs*? Another thing of significance to me is the memory of my childhood and being reared in a small East Tennessee town. I was a skinny kid. The most poignant, intense memory of being a skinny kid was walking by the forbidden ROYAL LUNCH ROOM, the most popular poolhall in our nearest town, Saturday morning, and smelling the wonderful, mouth-watering aroma of the magnificent chili dogs they served there. Hot dogs still symbolize to me an era of innocence.

Supper At Mama's? That is another important aspect of a man's life—relationships. After we settle our relationship with God, the only things we will take out of this world and into eternity are our bonds to each other, the character we develop, and our good works.

Many evenings Mama will have fixed supper and the family will sit in her living room with all the lights off and "watch it get dark in the corners," talking quietly of things that have happened and things to come; gently building and solidifying relationships.

Thus the idea of *God's Grace, Chili Dogs & Supper At Mama's* was born. I hope the reading of it is as enjoyable as was the writing.

There are some basic things that must be addressed before we get to the food: cooking stuff. I strongly recommend you purchase an oven thermometer. One can be had for less than five dollars and the benefit gained is well worth the small expense. Put it into your oven and set the temperature dial to 400 degrees, wait about ½ hour, and then check the thermometer. Note the difference and in the future add or deduct an appropriate amount when setting the temperature dial.

Many recipes here are very old and call for double-acting baking powder. You may use any of today's modern baking powder as purchased off the grocery shelf.

By definition, shortening is solid at room temperature; oil is liquid at room temperature. If the recipe calls for shortening, do not substitute cooking oil.

Many of Mama's recipes had to be converted from "dashes of" and "a little of" measurements, mostly in seasonings. Always use your own taste and judgment when adding salt and spices. Also, when one of her recipes calls for "a teacup" use a teacup and not an official one-cup measure.

You will find references to "a WOODSON'S bag full." WOODSON'S SHOPPING CENTER was opened in about 1958 or 1959 and was our very first shift from the small grocery store to a large shopping hub of highly visible, aisle shopping. Their paper grocery bags, although standard size, were heavy, strong, and distinctly printed with bold red on white. Luggage was scarce, and the "WOODSON'S bag" became our universal carry-all. I have personally seen travelers carrying this distinctive hand luggage as far away as Atlanta. One lady says she spotted one in Detroit.

Many recipes, because of their age are less than specific about canning procedures. For the sake of safety, always use modern, standard canning methods. The *Ball Blue Book*, published by the BALL CORPORATION, Muncie, Indiana, is an excellent resource and includes reliable and up-to-date home canning techniques.

Generally speaking, when a recipe calls for flour and does not specify all-purpose (plain) or self-rising, use all-purpose if it also lists baking powder and salt in the ingredients.

There are many foods that cannot be cooked without a cast-iron, black skillet. A brand new one, however, must first be "broken in" or seasoned. Most new ones will have instructions on how to do this; if not, phone a good cook who is over sixty and ask how it is done. Better yet, borrow one from someone's Mama or Grandmama.

This is not a low-fat, low-cholesterol cookbook. A steady diet of many of the dishes here would probably not be healthy, but an occasional, prudent step back into the history of cookery in our Appalachian region and a recollection of a more slow and gentle time might make up for the additional calories.

There are several recipes at the end of this book that are not of traditional Appalachian origin, and perhaps not even Southern; they are simply some that I like very well. I hope you enjoy these too.

Finally, if you look for any logic in the placement of the recipes here, you will be shot. I placed them as my fancy was tickled. You will not find them grouped according to types of food, as deserts, main dishes, etc., but may find tomato gravy beside fresh coconut cake, or pot roast next to peach cobbler. There are many times I grouped dishes very loosely according to the season, and some times put recipes together according to menu. Sometimes I placed them because they looked nice that way. *Use the index freely.*

'Cause Cookin's lak religion is—
   Some's 'lected and some ain't,
An' rules don' no mo' mek a cook
   Den sermons mek a saint.

From "Bandanna Ballads"
By Howard Weeden

THE OLD MAN, THE BOY
AND TOMATOES

He makes me lie down in green pastures, he leads me beside quiet waters . . . Psalms 23:2

For I am the Lord, your God, who takes hold of your right hand and says to you, Do not fear; I will help you. Isaiah 41:13

THE BOY LOOKED DOWN the track and saw that his grandfather was getting ahead of him. It was hard to walk on the rail without falling off, and completely impossible to keep up with the long strides of the tall man walking in front. It was even difficult to keep up when he was just walking on the crossties. He would walk about five steps, and they were giant steps because the ties were almost two feet apart, and then quickly run to catch up and start the process over.

It was 1951 and the boy was five, almost six. He, Sister, Mama and Daddy lived just across the little branch that ran from the spring and down the hollow and separated their house from the home of his grandmother and grandfather, Granny and Daddy Bill.

Both places were owned by the "Association" as was

the plot of land about a mile away from the houses where the old man tended a garden. He and the boy would walk there each morning. The grandfather would work in the garden and the boy would play near the creek until it got near noon when they would walk back, sometimes carrying produce from the garden to use for the noontime meal they called dinner. The evening meal was supper. Today they would bring back a bushel of ripe tomatoes to be canned or made into juice.

Both the road and the railroad ran from the houses to alongside the garden, but the road was unpaved and dusty, especially when the infrequent car passed, so they usually walked the railroad.

The boy knew he would have to jump down from the rail on which he was trying to stay balanced to catch up to the man pretty soon, because just around the next curve was the trestle that crossed the creek. His grandfather would pick him up and carry him across, for it was very high, and especially scary when one looked down between the crossties to the roaring creek and rocks below. It could be that the bridge was not actually as high, nor the creek as foreboding as the boy thought, however it is not always fact, but impression that makes the real difference in fear. The boy rarely looked down as they crossed. He saw no good reason to become more scared if there was no need.

There would come a time when the boy would be the same age as the old man, although he would not then think of 47 as very old at all. There would be other trestles to cross also, ones that were even more scary than the one here. He would then realize the old man and his strong arms were just a paradigm to teach him early that the strong arms of God's grace are necessary. He would learn the lesson better too that fear is largely perception, for those who are aware of the strong arms of God's grace.

16

He looked up and saw that the man had stopped and was waiting for him at a small branch that flowed through a culvert under the railroad to join the creek that ran parallel to it.

When the boy came up to him, he was squatted down whittling on a stick and tossing the shavings into the brook.

"Hot ain't it, Daddy Bill?"

"Yep. Not as hot as it's going to be though. We better hurry on up so we can get those tomatoes your Granny wants."

"Where's this water go to?" The boy had caught his breath now, and it was quiet; just an occasional bird singing flute-like three and four note songs about something it had seen yesterday.

"Well, I don't know for sure. It goes under here and to the creek and I guess it goes on somewhere to another bigger creek. Seems like I've heard somewhere that it finally ends up in the ocean, but I don't know for sure."

"Where'd it come from then?"

"You ask a lot of questions, you know that? But I can answer that one. Just be real quite. Listen to it."

They both squatted there listening. Even the bird hushed. The stream began making noises no one usually heard unless they made a special effort for quietness. The water hissed and gurgled. It reminded the boy of the satisfying sound the morning bacon made when his Mama put it in the skillet on her wood stove. Sometimes when it rained, and the windows were up just a little bit and he pressed his nose to the rusty screen there was a special sound its gentle fall made as it washed the leaves of the trees. It was sort of like the sound the rocker made on the front porch while Granny rocked and no one was talking.

"You hear that boy? That music the water's making?

What it's doing is telling you where it's been. You just have to listen real hard."

He stood, closed the knife, put it in his pocket, tossed the stick into the stream and picked the boy up.

"We better get on to the garden. Your Granny wants to get started on those tomatoes"

Tomato Juice

4 Gallons
  Completely Ripe
  Tomatoes
6-8 Large Sweet
  Green Peppers
6-8 Large Onions
1 Large Bunch
  Celery
Salt
Sugar

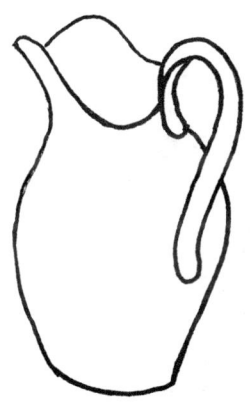

Wash the tomatoes and cut off the stem end and bottom, but do not peel. Quarter the tomatoes into a large kettle. Remove the stem end and seeds from the peppers and cut them into chunks, clean and quarter the onions, clean and string the celery but keep the leaf ends, and cut the celery stalks into two or three-inch pieces. Add all these vegetables to the quartered tomatoes and mix well. Add just enough water (about four cups) to allow the mixture to boil. When the mixture begins to boil, stir it to keep it from sticking. When cooking well, reduce the heat, cover and simmer until all the ingredients are tender.

Remove from the heat and force the resulting mix through a FOLEY food mill. Discard anything that does not go through the mill. Pour the resulting juice and pulp into a large pot, bring to a boil and then carefully pour it into hot, clean quart jars. Add one teaspoon salt and one teaspoon sugar and any other preferred seasoning to each jar. Place lids and rings on the jars and process in a pressure cooker at fifteen pounds of pressure for 30 minutes.

Tomato Sauce

2 Gallons Ripe Tomatoes
6 Large Sweet Green Peppers
6 Large Onions
2 Tablespoons Salt
1½ Cups Sugar
1½ Cups Brown Sugar
1 Cup Apple Cider Vinegar
2 Tablespoons Pickling Spice
   (Wrapped In A White Cloth
   And Tied, Or Use A Tea
   Caddie)
½-1 Teaspoon Cayenne Pepper
   (Optional)

Peel and quarter the tomatoes, seed and chop the peppers, and chop the onions. In a large kettle mix and cook all the ingredients rapidly until the mixture is reduced by half. Lower the heat and simmer until thick. Pour into clean, hot, pint jars, seal and process in a pressure cooker at fifteen pounds for ten minutes.

Mama makes this sauce every summer that we can find lots of tomatoes. When we grow them in the garden in the back yard, it is rare to have many ripen at once; usually we get 8-10 at a time.

Fortunately, there are lots of commercial farms in Cocke County and up around Lowland. When they have finished picking for the summer, if you can locate farmers who still have tomatoes on their vines, they will allow you to pick your own for about $6.00 a bushel.

Use the sauce in meat loaf, baked beans, or as a base for barbecue sauce.

20

This is a depression era recipe given to me by Ken and Jean Neidig. Ken was reared in a very small community in Pennsylvania that consisted of about six families. He said there were six houses, two Churches, a one-roomed school and a blacksmith shop. All the social activities of the little community focused around the two Churches.

TOMATO CAKES

1 Pint Canned Tomatoes
3 Slices Stale Bread, Crumbled
2 Teaspoons Baking Powder
1 Small Onion, Chopped Fine
½-1 Cup Flour
Cooking Oil In An Iron Skillet

Mix the first four ingredients and add enough flour to make the mixture stiff, just slightly thicker than the consistency of pancake batter. Heat a little oil in an iron skillet on the stove top. Drop one tablespoonful of batter at a time into the hot grease in the skillet, browning both sides.

TOMATO PUDDING

1 Quart Canned Tomatoes With
   Juice
6 Left-Over Biscuits, Crumbled
½ Cup Sugar
½ Teaspoon Salt
2 Tablespoons Butter

Empty the canned tomatoes and their juice into a saucepan and bring to the boiling point. Add the crumbled biscuits, sugar, salt and butter. Cook at medium-high, stirring occasionally, until thick. Serve with almost any meal as you would sawmill gravy. Store-bought canned tomatoes may still have their cores. If so, remove them before using the tomatoes.

The tomato is my number one, favorite vegetable. Well, my favorite fruit.

Technically, it is a fruit, *Lycopersicon Esuientum,* but cultivated and used as a vegetable.

Until the beginning of this century it was thought to be poisonous, though helped from that stigma somewhat by Thomas Jefferson who grew them on his farm at Monticello.

Fried Green Tomatoes

Pat has a hard time when she fixes these in the early summer. After a long tomato-less winter, this is usually the first product from the garden except for tiny green onions. It is sort of like frying oysters; you can only do a few at a time, and the first batch is usually eaten before the second batch is done.

5-6 Large Green Tomatoes
Corn Meal
1-2 Eggs, Beaten
Salt
Bacon Grease or Cooking Oil

Remove the stem and blossom ends and cores of the tomatoes. Cut crosswise into slices about ¼-inch thick. Sprinkle lightly with salt. Dip each slice in egg, and then both sides of each slice, individually into corn meal.

Heat about two-three table-spoons of bacon drippings or oil in a heavy cast-iron skillet. Place the tomatoes in a single layer in the fat and fry at medium heat until they brown on the bottom. Turn with a small spatula and brown the other side. Continue to fry in this manner until all the slices are finished.

MARINATED TOMATO SLAW

½ Head Cabbage, Finely Grated
1 Large Sweet Pepper, Cut
   Crosswise Into Rings
1 Large Onion, Separated Into
   Rings
2 Medium Tomatoes, Cubed
½ Teaspoon Ground Cloves
½ Teaspoon Cinnamon
¾ Cup Vinegar
¾ Cup Granulated Sugar
1 Teaspoon Salt
¼ Teaspoon Black Pepper

Into a large bowl, add the grated cabbage and then green pepper, onion rings and tomatoes. Do not mix together at this time. Mix the next five ingredients and pour over the slaw mixture and blend lightly. Marinate at least one hour, covered in the refrigerator before serving, longer if possible.

I have never seen this dish in any other cookbook, and believe it may be original with Mama's grandmother who handed it down to my grandmother, Bess.

Having a sweet-sour taste, it compliments almost any meat, especially pork roast.

If you try no other recipe in this book, fix this one.

24

Mama Laura's Tomato Gravy

¾ Pound Pork Sausage
4 Tablespoons Flour
1 Can Tomatoes With Juice (28 Ounce)
½ Teaspoon Garlic Powder
½ Teaspoon Onion Salt
½ Teaspoon Mexene Chili Powder
⅛ Teaspoon Ground Black Pepper
¼ Teaspoon Salt

In a ten-inch cast-iron skillet, fry the sausage into about eight-ten patties. Drain and reserve the pan drippings. Scrape the skillet, loosening any bits of fat and meat. To the scrapings add back 3½ tablespoons of the reserved pan drippings. Reduce the heat to medium-low and add four tablespoons of flour. Stir the flour and drippings for about one minute. Add the tomatoes; slowly because the skillet is hot. If the tomatoes are whole, break them apart with a spatula. Add the spices and stir. Once the meat was removed, the above process should have taken about five minutes to accomplish. Now would be a good time to put your biscuits into a preheated oven to brown. As the biscuits bake, cook the gravy for an additional ten minutes, stirring occasionally. Serve as an accompaniment to the biscuits, sausage and scrambled eggs. If you have no aversion to MSG, add about ½ teaspoon of Accent when you add the spices. Yield: about four servings.

Mama Laura was Pat's father's mother.

25

1 Peck Green Tomatoes (About
   18, Or 2 Gallons)
1 Quart Sliced Apples
1 Pound Seedless Raisins
½ Cup Salt
1 Pound Suet, Chopped
2 Teaspoon Cinnamon
2 Teaspoon Nutmeg
2 Teaspoon Ground Cloves
2½ Pounds Brown Sugar
3 Lemons

Wash the tomatoes and cut them into small pieces. Sprinkle with ½ cup salt and let them stand, covered, overnight. Drain and pour clean water over the tomatoes and drain them again. Add sufficient water to prevent sticking and cook for 30 minutes, stirring often. Add the juice of 3 lemons and the grated rind of 1 lemon and the white of 1 lemon, cut into small pieces. Add the apples, suet, raisins and sugar. Add spices to taste and a dash of salt if needed. Simmer slowly, stirring often, until the tomatoes and apples are tender and the flavors blend. Pack into freshly sterilized jars and seal, using the standard hot-water bath canning method.

Then their father Israel said to them, "If it must be, then do this: Put some of the best products of the land in your bags and take them down to the man as a gift—a little balm and a little honey, some spices and myrrh, some pistachio nuts and almonds. . ." Genesis 43:11

5 Pounds Tomatoes (11 Cups
    Quartered)
4-5 Pounds Sugar
Grated Rind And Juice Of 3
    Lemons
2 Tablespoons Cinnamon

If they are available, substitute yellow tomatoes for red. This will give surprisingly good results and color.

Scald, peel and quarter the tomatoes. Add sugar, cover with a clean cloth and let stand overnight at room temperature. The next morning, drain the juice into a pan of sufficient size, bring it to a boil and then boil rapidly until the juice will spin a thread (about 230 degrees). Add the tomatoes, rind, lemon juice and cinnamon. Return to a boil and continue boiling until the preserves are thick and clear. Use the hot-water bath canning method to preserve in small glass jars.

Serve this as with any preserves, it is especially tasty with pork. Mama says that "spin a thread" means to dip a spoonful of the mixture from the pot as it is cooking. Let a little of it drip back into the pot. If the mixture forms a thread as it drips, then it has cooked enough.

POKE WITH EGGS

Fresh, Small Poke, (About ½ A
  Woodson's Bag Full)
3-5 Pieces Thick Bacon,
  (Smoked Hog Jowl Is Good)
2 Eggs, Well Beaten

Wash and prepare the poke as you would greens. Place them in a large pot and cover with water. Bring to a boil and continue to cook for ten minutes and then drain. In an iron skillet, fry the bacon. Remove the bacon and in the resulting drippings, cook the poke until it just starts to become dry, stirring frequently. Stir in the eggs and allow them to cook until just set, stirring constantly to keep from sticking. Serve with fried potatoes, sliced onions, hog jowl, cornbread and cold buttermilk. Yum-yum.

Tomatoes had the reputation for being poisonous until the beginning of this century. Poke *is* poisonous if eaten raw.

A.J. moved to our town from somewhere "up North" and lived just down the road from us. We roamed the hills and woods together, and one day picked some poke for Mama. A.J. took some of it home for his mother, and told her of the salad (pronounced *salit*) we were fixing. Just in time, Mama sent me to tell them not to eat it raw.

A.J. didn't get to play with me much after that.

28

WILTED LETTUCE AND GREEN ONIONS

This is also good with young mustard greens, or ½ mustard and ½ lettuce. Serve with fried cornbread. Daddy called this "poor man's caviar." Some call it "killed" or "kilt" lettuce. Do not substitute vegetable oil for the bacon drippings, although lard might be used.

1 Pound Tender Young Leaf
   Lettuce
6 Medium Green Onions With
   Tops
½ Cup Bacon Drippings
1 Tablespoon Vinegar
1 Tablespoon Sugar

Wash the onions and lettuce, tearing the lettuce into bite-sized pieces, and chopping both the onions and their tops. Place the lettuce and onions in a heat-proof serving dish. In a heavy cast-iron skillet heat the bacon drippings until very hot. Stir in vinegar and sugar. Pour this mixture over the lettuce and onions, mix well and serve at once.

Freshly Picked Greens (About A
Woodson's Bag Full)
Turnip, Mustard, Kale or
Collards, Or A Combination
Ham Hocks, Or Other Seasoning
Meat

Wash the greens thoroughly, using at least three changes of water. Pick over the greens to remove move any stray stems or bad looking pieces. Place the greens in a large pot about ⅓ full of water and add the seasoning meat. Cover and bring to a full boil. Reduce the heat, but not enough to stop the boiling. Cook covered until tender. Taste and add salt if necessary. Remove the lid and cook an additional fifteen minutes. Serve with the liquid.

If you use a left-over or pre-cooked ham hock, put it into the water in the pot before putting the greens in. Cook covered, at medium heat about 30 minutes. If the ham is not precooked, then cook covered for about 1½ hours, or until the meat is done and tender. Remove the meat from the liquid, add enough water to bring the liquid to ⅓ potful add cleaned, rinsed greens, and cook covered until tender. Add the meat back to the liquid and greens, taste and add salt if necessary and cook uncovered for an additional ten-fifteen minutes.

I must admit that I cannot recall ever eating dandelion greens, although Mama says she has fixed them often. Like poke weed, they were considered a healthy spring tonic. Pick the greens before the plant blooms or they will be tough and quite bitter.

Other edible wild greens are miner's lettuce, wild mustard, plantains, sorrel, cress and chickweed. Be absolutely positive concerning identification before eating any wild green, as some could prove poisonous.

DANDELION GREENS

½ WOODSON'S Bag Dandelion Leaves
Butter
Salt
Vinegar
Pepper

Pick the greens in the very early spring while they are still pale in color. Pick the grocery bag full if you just fill it loosely. If you press them down, however and pack them into the bag, you should need only about ½ a bag. Wash the dandelion leaves thoroughly, trimming as necessary. Place them in a large pot in about one inch of boiling water. Cook for one minute, or until the greens are wilted. Drain and replace with fresh water. Stir, and continue to cook, covered, until tender, about one hour. Drain and season with butter, salt, pepper and vinegar.

Dandelion Recipe

One Quart (Full And
    Overflowing) Dandelion
    Blossoms
1 Gallon Boiling Water
3 Oranges Sliced and Seeded
3 Lemons, Sliced and Seeded
3 Pounds Granulated Sugar
1 Yeast Cake (Or one package)
1 Pound Raisins

No longer drink only water, but use a little wine for your stomach's sake and your frequent infirmities. 1 Timothy 5:23

Look over the dandelions and remove anything green; you want only yellow flowers, nothing green. Wash the blossoms and cover with the gallon of boiling water. Let the mixture stand for 24 hours, then strain and add the other ingredients. Let this concoction stand for four days or a week, stirring each day, then strain again and bottle.

Put the bottles away and forget them until about Thanksgiving, then strain the mixture through filter paper and re-bottle.

I have ordered fried okra in restaurants and have been served some sort of breaded concoction that seemed to have been put into the french fry basket and deep fried. That is not my idea of fried okra. Some things you just have to do yourself if you expect it to be done right.

4 Good Handsful of Fresh Okra
½-1 Teaspoon Salt
½ Cup Flour
½ Cup Corn Meal
Shortening

Wash young, tender okra and cut off and discard the ends. Slice crossway into about ¼-inch pieces. Combine salt, flour and corn meal in a paper bag. Now put in the okra and shake vigorously, coating each piece thoroughly. In a large iron skillet heat about ¼-inch of shortening until it is melted and very hot. Reduce the heat and fry the okra until it is well browned and crisp. Be sure to stir and turn as it cooks. You may not be able to get all the okra into the skillet at once. The okra will absorb the oil as it cooks. Add more oil as you fry additional okra. This will produce a crisp, crunchy okra that is good with any country meal.

Fried Cabbage

1 Small Head Cabbage
1 Small Bell Pepper
¼ Cup Cooking Oil or Bacon
   Drippings
½ Teaspoon Salt To Taste
1 Cup Water

Shred the cabbage with a sharp knife (do not chop), cut the pepper into small strips and add to the cabbage. Heat the oil in a large cast-iron skillet to medium. Add the cabbage, pepper, salt and water. Cover tightly and cook until all the liquid is gone. Remove the lid and fry slowly, stirring often until the cabbage begins to brown slightly. Serve at once. For a slightly more German taste, add a pinch of caraway seeds.

The onion, mentioned only one time in the Bible, never-the-less must have made a significant impression on the children of Israel. Along with garlic and leeks, it was one of the flavor-full things they desperately missed during their wilderness journey.

Tom T. Hall wrote a song awhile back that told of some of the things he loves. Along with "old pickup trucks" he wrote, ". . . and onions."

What would we do without them?

BAKED WHOLE ONIONS

6 Medium Sized Onions,
    Washed But Not Peeled
Melted Butter
Salt
Paprika
Parmesan Cheese

Wash the onions, but do not remove the outer peel or cut the top or bottom. Place onions on a rack in a pan holding about ¼-inch water and bake in a 375 degree oven for about 1½ hours. When baked, slice off the root end and discard the outer shells. Place in a serving bowl and pour the melted butter over the baked onions, season with salt and paprika and sprinkle with grated Parmesan cheese.

CREAMED ONIONS

8 Walnut-Sized Onions (Or Cut
    Larger Ones In Half)
¾ Teaspoon salt
½ Stick Butter (¼ Cup)
2 Tablespoons Flour
1 Teacup Evaporated Milk

Place the peeled onions in a pot, cover with water, add salt and cook until tender, about ½ hour, and then add butter. In a teacup, measure two tablespoons of flour and add just enough evaporated milk to make a stiff paste with no lumps. Finish filling the teacup with evaporated milk and blend with the paste. Bring the onions to a boil and gradually add the flour-milk mixture. Mix and cook over medium heat until you have a thick gravy. Serve as a vegetable side dish. Yield: four servings.

We remember the fish we ate in Egypt at no cost—also the cucumbers, melons, leeks, onions and garlic. Numbers 11:5

36

Job had an interesting comment on boiled eggs. He recognized that its flavor comes from the yolk and without it wasn't of much use as savory food.

Fortunately, these retain their yolks and have salt as one of the seasonings. Serve them alongside almost any entree.

Is tasteless food eaten without salt, or is there flavor in the white of an egg?
Job 6:6

6 Eggs, Hard Boiled And Sliced
1 Cup Water
¾ Teaspoon salt
½ Stick Butter (¼ Cup)
2 Tablespoons Flour
1 Teacup Evaporated Milk

In a saucepan bring the water and salt to a boil and then add butter. In a teacup, measure two tablespoons of flour and add just enough evaporated milk to make a stiff paste with no lumps. Finish filling the teacup with evaporated milk and blend with the paste. Gradually add the flour-milk mixture. Reduce the heat to medium and cook until the sauce is like a thick gravy. Arrange sliced boiled eggs in a serving dish and cover with the cream sauce. Use as a side dish. Yield: four servings.

CINCINNATI FISH
WITH GRAVY

Salt Pork
1½ Cups Corn Meal
2 Tablespoons Shortening

Slice salt pork about ⅛-inch thick and roll in cornmeal. In a cast-iron skillet, heat the shortening and lightly brown the meat on both sides. Remove the pork and leave about two tablespoons of drippings in the skillet. Add 1½ tablespoons additional corn meal and brown, stirring constantly. Add one pint of water and cook mixture until thick, stirring constantly. Serve the meat and gravy with fried eggs and *Angel Biscuits*.

During the depression era, especially in towns where families could not raise a garden or have livestock, many could not afford expensive cuts of beef. Salt pork, cheap and readily available was widely used, and fixed in numerous ways.

Sliced thinly and fried, then covered with gravy it resembled pan-fried fish.

FRIED COUNTRY HAM WITH RED-EYE GRAVY

Sliced Country
   Ham
Cooking Oil Or
   Bacon Drippings
½ Cup Strong,
   Black Coffee

Mama says that the worst thing you can do to good country ham is to cook it too long. It becomes hard and tough. Her Mama said that when the fat on the edges had browned, it was time to turn it over and cook the other side. When the fat on the second side browned, it was time to eat.

Purchase or have your butcher slice Tennessee or Kentucky country ham to about ¼-inch thick. Place the slices in a shallow dish, cover with milk and let soak for about an hour. Remove the ham and drain and then pat dry with paper towels. Put just a little bit of oil into a large cast-iron skillet and heat to medium. Add the ham and cook each side for about five minutes. Do not overcook or the ham will become hard. Test the tenderness with a fork. After all the ham has cooked, remove the meat and scrape the bits of fat and ham from the bottom of the skillet and slowly add about ½ cup black coffee. Stir, scraping the pan, for about a minute. Pour two tablespoons of the resulting red-eye gravy over the ham slices on a serving dish and offer the rest in a small dish. Serve with eggs, biscuits, and molasses or honey. Red-eye gravy makes a wonderful biscuit "sop" when mixed equally with molasses.

Fat Back In Gravy

1 Pound Salt Pork
1 Quart Water
2 Cups Cornmeal
2 Tablespoons Onion, Chopped
2 Tablespoons Flour
1 Cup Milk

Bring the quart of water to a boil and into the boiling water dip the salt pork which has been thinly sliced. Drain the pork and dip the slices in cornmeal to coat. Brown slowly in a cast-iron skillet over medium heat, turning often until the meat has cooked through. Remove the meat and all but two tablespoons of the pan drippings. Add the chopped onions and sauté until golden. Now, add the flour and brown to a light tan. Slowly blend in the milk and stir, cooking until thick. Serve with fried eggs, grits and biscuits.

It isn't something you would want to eat every day, because of the high saturated fat, but if you are from the South, this dish will recall a part of your culinary heritage.

Mama used to keep a covered metal can on the back of the stove, into which she would empty all the fat cooked out of any bacon. These drippings were used as a substitute for shortening or lard. Little else was available to her mother, except lard, and it did not have the same flavor.

You will notice modern canning instructions in this recipe. The way Mama gave it to me, though, was entirely without any heat processing except for precooking the sausage patties. Preservation was accomplished solely through sterilizing the jars and the air-tight seal provided by pouring the liquid fat in the jars and then storing them upside down.

CANNED PORK SAUSAGE

3 Pounds Freshly Made Pork Sausage

Use freshly ground sausage seasoned with salt, pepper, sage and red pepper flakes. Shape into patties and fry in an iron skillet until done and brown on both sides. Pack the cooked patties into hot, quart canning jars. Pour one inch only of the hot fat that cooked out of the meat over the sausage, seal and process in a pressure cooker at ten pounds for an hour and thirty minutes. When finished, stand jars upside down until completely cool and then store upside down. By turning upside down, the warm fat runs to the top of the jar and solidifies, thereby creating an additional seal.

When serving, simply remove sausage from jars and heat through in a skillet.

41

1-2 Pounds Fresh Pork

Ask your butcher for a piece of fresh, uncured pork with a lot of fat on it, or ask for some of the fat that gets trimmed off fresh pork. Dice the meat to about ¾-inch squares and put it on the stove top in a heavy pan over medium heat. Stir the cubes until grease starts to cook out of the meat and it starts to fry. Turn the heat to low or just a bit above low and cook slowly. Soon the pieces of fat will start to become very lightly browned. When the pieces of meat are brown, dip them out of the grease with a slotted spoon and drain the Cracklings thoroughly. The best method is to put them in some sort of stainer or colander over another container. To make cracklin' bread, chop the pieces a little smaller and simply add about a cup of them to your cornbread recipe.

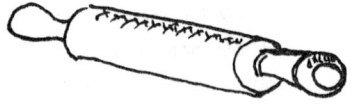

If you make your own Cracklings, as in this recipe, that which is left over is rendered lard. You can use it for lye soap, or for cooking.

Lye can be purchased at any grocery, but Granny Bess got hers from the wood stove ashes. Lye made in this way is know as potash and is less caustic than commercial lye. Any hardwood ash will do, but oak, hickory and maple are best.

The general process is to put the ashes into a wooden container with a small hole in the bottom, fill the container with water, and allow the liquid to leach out the potash. She would test it by cracking an egg into the solution. If the egg would barley float, it was ready.

LYE SOAP

5 Pounds Fat
1 Can Lye (1 Pound)
1 Quart Water, Plus ½ Cup
3 Teaspoons Borax
1 Teaspoon Salt
2 Tablespoons Sugar
¼ Cup Ammonia

Use fat scraps from hog killing, or ask your butcher for pork fat discards. Melt the fat and strain through folded cheesecloth. Dissolve the lye in the ½ cup cold water and then let it stand until it cools. When the lye-water mixture cools, add it slowly to the melted fat, stirring constantly. In a separate container, combine all the other ingredients and mix into the fat-lye mixture. Stir the whole thing until thick and light in color. Pour the mixture into a shallow pan lined with cloth. When the soap hardens break it into pieces and store in such a way that the soap may dry.

PICKLE RELISH

7-8 Cups Onions   6 Large Green Bell Peppers
1 Medium Cabbage (4 Cups)   10 Green Tomatoes
6 Red Sweet Peppers (Or 2 Jars Sliced Pimentos,
Drained, 7 Ounce Size)

In a large metal container (Mama uses a three gallon stock pot), chop each ingredient separately (if you use pimentos, these are not added at this time.) As each single ingredient is chopped to a medium texture, add it to a non-metal bowl. Make sure the bowl is large enough to hold approximately 10-12 pints. Mix lightly and sprinkle ½ cup salt (non iodized) over the top of the chopped mixture (don't stir), cover with a clean cloth and let stand overnight at room temperature.

The next morning, rinse and drain the relish combination. If you use pimentos instead of red sweet peppers, add them at this time. In a large pot (big enough to cook the above mixture) mix and bring to a boil the following ingredients:

4 Cups Apple Cider Vinegar   1½ Teaspoon Turmeric
2 Cups Water   1 Tablespoon Celery Seed
6 Cups Sugar   2 Tablespoons Mustard Seed

After the mixture begins to boil, add the drained and rinsed relish. Allow it to return to a boil, lower the heat and simmer for 3 minutes. After simmering, pack the relish into sterilized hot pint jars, being sure to include sufficient liquid to cover the relish in each jar. Use the hot water canning method to insure a proper seal. This is a light and dark green relish, sprinkled with bits of red. It has a fresh sweet-sour taste that compliments dishes like mettwurst and beans, and pintos with cornbread. It is also excellent used as an ingredient when making potato salad and deviled eggs, and can be used as hot-dog relish.

Mama fixed pinto beans every Monday, because that was wash day.

When she was a girl, there were no washing and drying machines and it was a long laborious process. Water had to be drawn from the well, carried to the house, heated over a wood fire, etc. You couldn't skip supper just because you were busy, so something nutritious and easy to fix was required.

Another method to use to prepare pinto beans is to allow them to soak in water overnight. You then drain the water, bring them to a boil, reduce the heat, add the meat and proceed as noted.

WASH DAY PINTO BEANS

1 Pound Dried Pinto Beans
8 Ounce Piece Salt Pork
    (Or Country Ham, Ham
    Shoulder Or Shank)
Salt

Wash and pick through the beans, removing any rocks and beans that look bad. Put the pintos into a pot, cover with water and bring to a boil. Immediately remove the beans from the heat and allow them to cool in the water. When cool, drain and again cover with water, return to stove, add meat (scored with a sharp knife but not cut through) and bring to a boil. Cover and cook about three hours. Stir occasionally and add water if it becomes too low. At the end of the three hour period remove about a cup of the beans, drain the liquid back into the pot, mash the cup of beans with a fork and return them to the pot. Cook for about another fifteen minutes. Just before serving, add salt. The beans may need as much as 1-3 teaspoons if the seasoning meat was not salty.

PICKLED STUFFED GREEN PEPPERS

Green Bell Peppers
(About 15-20)
1 Quart Chopped Onions
2 Tablespoons Mustard
2 Cups Vinegar
1 Small-Medium Head
Cabbage
1 Jar Chopped Pimentos
(4 Ounce)
½ Cup Brown Sugar
1 Teaspoon Ground
Black Pepper
1 Teaspoon Allspice

Select large firm peppers, cut off and save the tops and remove the seeds. Shred the cabbage head and combine with pimentos, onions, vinegar, mustard, sugar, pepper and spice and heat to boiling. Stuff the peppers firmly with this mixture. Sew the tops back on the peppers and pack into quart jars. Cover with vinegar which has been diluted one part vinegar to two parts water. This is a very old recipe, and I doubt many would be inclined to sew the tops back onto the peppers.

Mama can remember her mother making these, and calling them Mangos. Instead of sewing the tops, she would tie them with clean, heavy string. She says they would eat them with pinto beans and pork.

The peppers were not canned in the normal way, but packed into a large stone crock and kept in a cool place and removed as needed.

I would recommend discarding the tops and packing as many stuffed peppers as possible, very tightly, into quart jars. The pressure from the tight packing should be sufficient to keep the vegetable mixture inside the pepper shells.

Pack the peppers in hot sterilized jars, wipe the rims, pour the vinegar mixture over the Mangos, put on the lids and rims, and hot bath process the jars for fifteen minutes.

You will find another recipe here that is more traditional: Sauerkraut. This one is very good, and much easier.

3 Cabbages
1 Gallon Water
1 Cup Sugar
1 Cup Salt
1 Cup Vinegar

Chop or grate the cabbage to the desired texture and pack into sterilized jars to within one-inch of top. Dissolve the sugar, salt and vinegar in water and pour this over the cabbage. Put lids and rings on the jars and process in a hot water canner for fifteen minutes for pints, and twenty minutes for quart jars. If you use medium size cabbages, this recipe makes about six pints of Kraut. Large cabbages will make almost 10 pints.

SAUERKRAUT

7-8 Heads Cabbage	5 Gallon Stone Crock
2¼ Pounds Canning Salt	12 Tart Apples

Select large, heavy cabbages. Remove and keep the outer leaves and then cut the cabbages into quarters, remove the cores and shred the quarters very small using a cabbage cutter. Into a large non-metal pan, place five pounds of the shredded cabbage. Sprinkle with ¼ cup salt, mix well and pack into the crock. Place one cup of the apples, chopped fine, on top of the cabbage. Using a round board that will fit into the crock, place the board on top of the mixture and using a broom handle, press down very firmly. Brine will flow out of the pressed mixture and cover the board. Remove the board, add another five pounds of cabbage and a cup of apples prepared in the same way, on top of the first layer. Press again. Continue to add layers until all the cabbage is used.

Using the leaves kept from the cabbage heads, cover the mixture in the crock. On top of the leaves, place a fitted square of clean cloth and weigh down with a plate, and on top of that place a large clean stone or brick to keep the contents under brine. Don't fill all the way to the top; it will swell.

Put the crock in a warm place to "work". In 2 weeks, remove the stone and plate and remove the scum that has collected. If you cautiously pick up the corners of the cloth, you can get most of the residue. Wash the cloth, dish, stone and sides of the crock with warm water and replace. Now, move the crock to a cool place.

It is now ready to use. If you keep the kraut in the stone crock, be sure to remove the cloth, etc. and clean weekly.

The fermented sauerkraut may be packed in glass jars. Pack into jars, cover with brine from the crock, heat thoroughly, using the hot water-bath canning method to seal.

Lots of trouble, isn't it? Recall how Jesus made the natural process of fermentation happen in an instant, using only water? Divine power over nature. John 2:8

FRIED MUSH

Left-Over Mush, Sliced
    Thin (About ½-Inch)
Butter
Syrup
1 Cup Plain Cornmeal
3 Cups Milk
1 Teaspoon Salt

To make the mush, bring the milk to a boil over medium heat and then slowly stir in the cornmeal. Cook for about six minutes, stirring constantly. The resulting mush will be very thick. Spoon it into a lightly greased loaf-like dish and refrigerate overnight.

For breakfast, melt butter in an iron skillet and slowly brown the thinly sliced mush on both sides. Serve with butter and syrup or sprinkled with powdered sugar. This may appear to be a quick breakfast, but it is not. To achieve the light golden, crisp outside that this needs, you should brown it very slowly, about seven-eight minutes on each side.

This dish, along with fat-back and gravy, was a winter staple for many families during the depression years, it probably was all that many families had on hand. It lasted well after the hard times though, because it was so tasty.

HOME-MADE SYRUP

3 Cups Sugar
⅓ Cup Water
1 Tablespoon Maple
    Extract

In a heavy pan, mix the sugar and water. Over medium heat bring the combination to a boil and stir constantly until the sugar has completely dissolved. Add the maple extract and serve warm over waffles or pancakes.

MAMA'S LIVER HASH

2-3 Pounds Pork Liver
1 Large Onion, Chopped
   Fine
2 Teaspoons Rubbed
   Sage
½-1 Teaspoon Salt
Black Pepper
Plain Cornmeal

Place the liver in a pan and add enough water to cover. Bring to a boil and continue cooking until the liver is cooked through, about 20 minutes. Remove the liver from the liquid, keeping the liquid. Crumble the cooked liver coarsely, removing any gristle. Add the onion and return the liver-onion mixture back to the reserved liquid. Simmer for 15 minutes. Add plain cornmeal, a little at-a-time, until the mixture is the consistency of cooked oatmeal. Add salt, pepper and sage to taste. Serve warm and refrigerate any unused portions. Use chilled with mayonnaise to make sandwiches the next day.

LIVER HASH

3 Pounds Pork Liver
½ Teaspoon Red Pepper
2 Teaspoons Sage
½-1 Teaspoon Salt
Rich Broth (Condensed
   Canned Is Okay)
Plain Cornmeal
Black Pepper

Use the same method to cook the liver in *Mama's Liver Hash*, except, discard the water in which the liver was cooked. Grind the meat fine. Add 1 cup of broth for each 2 cups of ground liver. Add a portion of the salt, red pepper, and sage. Mix well and taste. Adjust the seasonings and add black pepper as desired. Add roughly ½ cup cornmeal for every 2 cups of broth you previously used. Bring the mixture to a boil and cook, stirring constantly until the mixture is thick. It will begin to pull away from the sides of the pan. Pack the hash firmly into a greased loaf pan. Chill and serve cold.

I've heard that Hoppin' John got its name from the children hopping around in the kitchen waiting for it to be done.

It is a starchy dish, and is traditional to be served on New Years Day to bring good luck throughout the year.

HOPPING JOHN

1 Cup Cooked Rice
2 Tablespoons Butter
2 Cups Dried Black-Eyed Peas
¼ Pound Peppered
    Side Meat, Or Salt Pork
Salt
Pepper
Butter

Soak the black-eyed peas overnight. The next day drain them, put the peas into a kettle and then add sufficient water to cover them, plus the pork, cut into two-inch pieces. Cook until the peas are soft, being careful to keep them whole during the cooking. When the peas are cooked and tender, there should be only a small quantity of liquid left in the pot. Remove the salt pork and mix the cooked rice, peas and the liquid from the peas together. Season with salt, pepper and butter.

51

FRIED CHICKEN LIVERS

10-15 Whole Chicken Livers
¾ Cup Flour
1 Teaspoon Salt
½ Teaspoon Freshly Ground
    Pepper
¾ Cup Oil
1 Tablespoon Water

Wash the livers and place them into a paper bag with the flour, salt and pepper. Shake the bag vigorously to coat the livers. Heat the oil in an iron skillet to medium-hot. Add the coated livers and cover as the oil will pop. Brown quickly on both sides, about five minutes. Turn the heat to off and add one tablespoon water. Cover tightly and allow to stand for fifteen minutes on the cooling stove eye before serving.

Except for goose livers, chicken livers are the most tender available, the next best being calves liver.

All types of liver are a valuable source of iron, Vitamin A, and B vitamins.

In Morristown, for excellent grilled calves liver smothered in onions visit the LITTLE DUTCH RESTAURANT on South Cumberland Street, and see George and Nina Angelos.

Roast Goose

It may seem harsh, but it was a less squeamish time. Mama said that to insure a nice fat goose, they would nail its feet to a board so it couldn't walk around. So constricted, all the food it was given was more likely to be converted to fat.

1 Nice Fat Goose
2 Tablespoons Ground Ginger
1 Large Onion
6 Whole Cloves
1 Cup Water
Salt
Pepper

Prepare and clean the goose just as you would a turkey, chicken or duck; rub with salt and pepper. Rub the two tablespoons of ground ginger on both the inside and outside of the goose. Stick the cloves into a peeled onion and place it inside the bird. Place the goose into a roaster, make a tent of aluminum foil and add one cup of water. Roast at about 325 degrees, basting often, adding water as necessary. When tender and done, remove the foil and brown until the skin is crisp. Use the drippings and make a highly seasoned gravy.

SCRAPPLE

2 Cups Ground Pork
2 Cups Ground Beef
3 Cups Meat Broth
1 Cup Cornmeal
2 Teaspoons Salt
½ Teaspoon Pepper
1½ Teaspoons Sage
Cayenne

Combine the meats and broth, heat to boiling, and add the seasonings. Sift in the cornmeal slowly, stirring constantly. Add a dash of cayenne and cook for 30 minutes. Pour the scrapple into an oiled mold and chill until firm. To serve, cut into thin slices and brown in oil.

Although this is a more modern version, the traditional mountain scrapple was near what the name sounds to be; scraps. It is a historic dish made from the scraps of hog butchering. The original was a popular, inexpensive family staple.

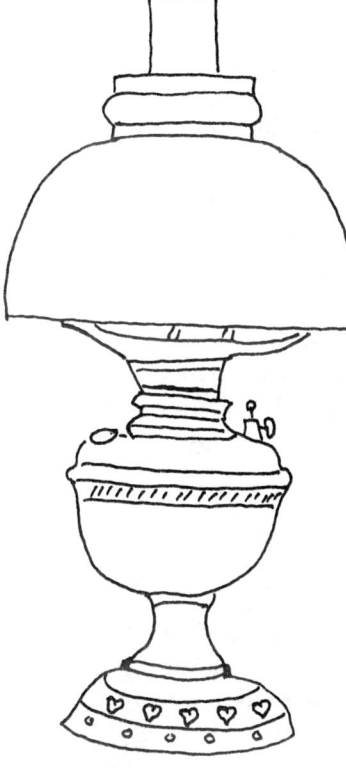

Hot Slaw

1 Quart Cabbage, Chopped Fine
1 Teaspoon Salt
¼ Teaspoon Pepper
1 Cup Mild Vinegar
½ Cup Sugar
2 Teaspoons Flour
1 Egg, Well Beaten
½ Cup Milk

In a mixing bowl, combine cabbage, salt and pepper. In a saucepan bring the vinegar to a boil and then add the sugar, flour, beaten egg, and milk. Return to a boil and then using a rotary hand beater, slowly beat until the mixture is the consistency of thick cream. Remove from the heat and let stand for three minutes and then mix well with the cabbage.

5 Cups Half & Half, Divided 4
   Cups And 1
⅓ Cup Cornmeal
¾ Cup Molasses
¼ Cup Butter
1 Teaspoon Salt
½ Teaspoon Ginger
3 Tablespoons Sugar
2 Small Eggs, Beaten
½ Cup Currents or Raisins
½ Teaspoon Cinnamon
¼ Teaspoon Nutmeg

Preheat oven to 300 degrees. Using a double boiler, heat water to boiling in the bottom half to use later. In the top half of the double boiler, sitting directly on a stove eye, heat the four cups half-and-half to boiling and then stir in the cornmeal. Put this mixture over the boiling water you fixed in the bottom half and cook it for about fifteen minutes. Now, stir in the molasses and cook an additional five minutes. Remove from the heat and stir in the butter, salt, ginger, egg, raisins, cinnamon and nutmeg. Pour this mixture into a well-greased baking dish.

Bake in the pre-heated oven for one hour. Remove the pudding from the oven and gently pour the remaining cup of half-and-half over the top *without* stirring. Return to the oven and cook an additional three hours (seems long, but the time is correct.) Adding the cold milk will cause the pudding to have a soft center. Serve the pudding hot with vanilla ice cream.

Mama's mother was one quarter Cherokee, so that makes me just a bit Native American. Perhaps that is why I enjoy this pudding so much.

2 eggs
1¾ Cups Boiling Water
¾ Cup Corn Meal
2 Tablespoons Butter
3 Eggs
1¼ Cup Milk
1 Teaspoon Salt
1 Teaspoon Baking Powder

Spoon bread is kin to tortillas and hush puppies, though a little more formal. We were served this at THE KING'S ARMS TAVERN in Colonial Williamsburg, so I suspect it has an English origin.
It is important that baking be discontinued while the bread is still moist. Serve by spoonsful.

Using a double boiler over simmering water, place corn meal in the top portion. Pour the 1¾ cups boiling water over the corn meal. Cook, stirring constantly for about five minutes or until the mixture is thick and smooth. Add the butter and stir until melted, remove from heat and allow to cool.

Grease a medium sized baking dish. Beat the eggs and add milk and salt. Stir the egg mixture into the cooled corn meal. Beat until blended, add the baking powder and beat again. Turn the blend into the greased baking dish. Bake in a 425 degree oven for 40-45 minutes, until firm, but still moist. This recipe serves four.

JOHNNY BULL PUDDING

1 Cup Beef Suet	1 Cup Sugar
3 Eggs, Separated	1½ Cups Chopped Pecans
1 Cup Half & Half	1½ Cups Stale Bread Crumbs
3 Tablespoons Brandy	2 Teaspoons Baking Powder

2 Cups Apples, Peeled, Sliced and Ground
2 Teaspoons Orange Rind, Grated
1 Teaspoon Freshly Ground Nutmeg

To the finely chopped beef suet, slowly stir in 1 cup sugar, beat in the 3 egg yolks and stir in the half-and-half and brandy. Using a food processor, grind the apples and add, and then add the pecans, orange rind and nutmeg. Now, combine the bread crumbs and baking powder and add. Blend well. Beat the egg whites and gently fold these in. Mold by hand into a large round ball and wrap in several layers of cheese cloth. In a large stock pot, add about 2 inches of water. Insert a rack or trivet to support the pudding over the water, cover tightly, bring to a boil, and when steam begins to escape from around the lid, reduce the heat to medium-low and steam for 4 hours. Add water as necessary. When done, remove carefully and allow to rest for at least 30 minutes. Serve with hard sauce or orange marmalade.

Mama's grandmother made this and her method was just a bit different. She sewed the molded pudding in a flour sack and place it *into* the boiling water. When it had cooked, it would be hung to dry for several days and then be sliced and served. One may also use pudding molds or cans to place on the rack. If you do this, grease the mold first and sprinkle with sugar. Fill the molds only ⅔ full. When finished cooking, remove the mold or can from the pot, remove the lids and allow to rest before unmolding.

Pineapple Upside Down Cake

2 Tablespoons
   Butter
½ Cup Brown
   Sugar
4 Canned
   Pineapple Slices,
   Halved
4 Maraschino
   Cherries, Halved
⅓ Cup Shortening
1¼ Cups Sifted All-
   Purpose Flour
½ Cup Sugar
2 Teaspoons
   Baking Powder
½ Teaspoon Salt
½ Cup Pineapple
   Syrup
½ Teaspoon
   Grated Lemon
   Peel
1 Egg

Melt the butter in an 8 x 8 x 2-inch ovenproof pan. Stir in the brown sugar and arrange the pineapples on top of this mixture, and place a cherry half in each hollow. In a separate bowl, stir the shortening until it is softened. Sift in the dry ingredients and the pineapple syrup, lemon peel and egg. Mix until all the flour is dampened and then beat vigorously for two minutes. Pour the resulting batter over the pineapples and bake in a moderate 350 degree oven for 30 to 35 minutes. Serve warm with whipped cream.

This recipe was hand written in the front of an old cook book I found, and in the upper corner were the words "1920 Version." This cake was probably made in a cast-iron skillet.

Brown Betty Pudding

½ Cup Brown Sugar
3 Cups Bread Crumbs
3 Tablespoons Butter
2 Cups Tart Apples, Peeled,
   Cored And Chopped
½ Teaspoon Nutmeg
½ Teaspoon Cinnamon

Into a buttered dish, put a layer of apples, sprinkle with a portion of the brown sugar, dot with bits of butter, and add a little of the cinnamon and nutmeg. Add layers in the same manner until all the ingredients (except the bread crumbs) are used up. Blanket the top of the pudding with bread crumbs and cook covered in a 400 degree oven for about 30 minutes. Uncover the dish and brown. Serve with whipped cream or ice-cream. Serves eight-ten.

This desert is sometimes called Scalloped Apples. Writing in her book AMERICAN COOKERY, around 1845, Amelia Simmons said, "If every boy in America planted an apple tree in some useless corner, and tended it carefully, the net saving would in time extinguish the public debt." Amelia did not foresee the public debt of 1994, but her idea had merit.

Try one of these varieties for this dish; Jonathan, Stayman, Winesap, or McIntosh.

SPONGE CAKE BATTER

¾ Cup Sugar, Sifted
4 Egg Yolks
1 Teaspoon Vanilla
¾ Cup Cake Flour, Sifted
¾ Teaspoon Baking Powder
½ Teaspoon Salt
4 Egg Whites

Have all the ingredients at room temperature. Beat the yolks until light in color. Add the sugar and beat until creamy. Add the vanilla. Sift together flour, baking powder and salt and add gradually to the egg mixture. Beat until smooth. Whip the egg whites until stiff but not dry and fold them into the batter.

JELLY ROLL

Sponge Cake Batter
½ Cup Powdered Sugar

Pour the batter onto a cookie sheet so that the resulting cake will bake to ½-inch thick. Bake and turn out on an appropriately sized towel on which powdered sugar has been generously sprinkled. Using the towel to help support it, roll the flexible cake into a roll and let cool about ½-hour. Unroll and spread with apple (or favorite) jelly. Roll again, fastening with tooth picks. Let stand one hour. Slice crossways.

Old Fashioned
Strawberry Shortcake

4 Cups Sifted All-Purpose Flour
2 Tablespoons Baking Powder
1 Teaspoon Salt
⅓ Cup Sugar
⅔ Cup Butter
2 Large Eggs, Beaten
1 Cup Milk (Approximately)
3 Pints Fresh Strawberries
½ Cup Sugar
1 Pint Whipping Cream,
    Whipped

Sift the first four ingredients together into a mixing bowl. Add butter and cut it into the dry mixture with a pastry blender or two table knives until the mixture resembles coarse crumbs. Pour beaten eggs into a measuring cup, and add milk to make 1½ cups. Gradually stir this into the flour mixture. Knead for about twenty seconds on a lightly floured surface. Divide the dough into three equal portions. Pat the dough into three greased, round nine-inch layer cake pans and bake in a pre-heated 450 degree oven for fifteen minutes or until done. Cool in the pans for ten minutes and then turn out onto wire racks to finish cooling.

Prepare and slice the berries, saving three or four of the whole berries to garnish the top of the cake. Mix the sliced berries with ½ cup sugar and let them stand for about 30 minutes.

Spread whipped cream and sliced berries between layers and over the top. Garnish with whole uncapped berries. Let the shortcake stand for at least fifteen minutes, refrigerated before serving.

I asked Tom Williams, a talented butcher where one could obtain beef suet. He said that it is basically the fat trimmed off good quality cuts of beef. He suggested that the meat department of just about any large grocery store could supply suet if they had several days notice.

2 Pounds Lean Beef, Chopped Fine
4 Pounds Apples
2½ Pounds Raisins
4 Cups Brown Sugar
½ Teaspoon Cloves
1¼ Teaspoons Nutmeg
Grape Juice or Cider
½ Pound Beef Suet, Ground
1½ Pounds Currants
½ Pound Citron, Ground
1½ Teaspoons Cinnamon
1 Teaspoon Mace
2 Teaspoons Salt
½ Cup Molasses

Pare, core and chop the apples, and combine them with remaining ingredients. Add cider or grape juice to moisten. Simmer the mixture until the meats and fruits are tender, and flavors are blended. Pack into freshly sterilized jars and seal, using hot-water bath canning method.

63

MINCE PIE

2 Packages Condensed
   Mincemeat (9 Ounce Packages)
2 Tablespoons Water
3 Cups Water
1 Large Egg Yolk
2 Teaspoons Sugar
9-Inch Unbaked Pastry For Pie
   (Top & Bottom)

Prepare the pastry bottom in a nine-inch piepan. In a saucepan, blend the mincemeat with three cups of water. Bring the mixture to a boil and cook for one minute, stirring constantly. Allow to cool and turn the mixture into the bottom pastry. Cover with the pastry top and cut a pleasing arrangement of slits near the center, and seal the edges. Mix the egg yolk with two tablespoons of water and brush over the surface of the pie. Sprinkle two teaspoons of sugar over the brushed surface. Bake in the lower part of a 425 degree oven for 30 minutes or until golden brown.

Mama makes mince pies every Thanksgiving and Christmas, but when she moved to Morristown from LaFollette, she discovered it was easier there than here.

Condensed Mincemeat, sold in a small box, is dry and one adds water to reconstitute it. The problem Mama encountered was finding a grocery store in Morristown that sold it.

Unable to buy it at her regular store, she called all the others in the area and was invariably transferred to the meat manager.

Times have changed. One butcher said there was no such animal as a mince, or if there was, they had never gotten one at his store.

2 Eggs
1½ Cups Sugar
 Plus 1 Cup
 Sugar, Separate
2 Tablespoons
 Melted Butter
1 Cup Buttermilk
½ Teaspoon salt
1 Teaspoon
 Nutmeg
1 Teaspoon Soda
2 Teaspoons
 Baking Powder
4 Cups Plain Flour
3 Teaspoons
 Cinnamon
CRISCO Shortening

Beat the eggs, add 1½ cups sugar, butter and buttermilk and mix well. In a separate bowl mix the salt, nutmeg, soda, baking powder and flour and combine the two mixtures. Turn the resulting dough onto a floured surface and knead lightly. Roll to ¼-inch thick and cut with a two-inch donut cutter.

In a large, heavy cast-iron skillet, or an electric frying pan heat about ¾-inches of CRISCO to about 360 degrees. Fry a few donuts at a time, turning until they are evenly browned. Place them on paper towels and allow to drain. Put one cup sugar and three-four teaspoons of cinnamon into a paper bag. Place three or four donuts at a time into the bag and shake to coat.

FRIED PIES

1½ Cups Shortening
3 Cups Flour
1 Egg, Beaten
1 Teaspoon Salt
5 Tablespoons Ice Water
1 Tablespoon Vinegar

FILLING

1 Package Dried Apples
¾ Cup Sugar
½ Teaspoon Cinnamon
½ Teaspoon Ground Cloves
½ Teaspoon Nutmeg

Prepare the filling by placing dried apples in a saucepan, cover with water and cook over medium heat until tender. Add sugar, cinnamon, cloves and nutmeg and continue to cook until thick. The filling may be used immediately, but is better if left overnight in the refrigerator.

Cut shortening into the flour with two table knives. Add salt, eggs, vinegar and enough ice water to make a dough that just sticks together. Knead lightly on a floured surface and roll ½ of the dough at-a-time to about ⅛-inch thick. Cut into circles using a saucer as a guide. Place about two-three large tablespoons of the cooked apples on ½ of the circle of dough and fold over. Seal the edges with a fork and pierce the top of the pie several times. Fry in hot oil in a heavy skillet until brown. Turn and brown the other side and drain on paper towels. Sprinkle with sugar.

CHILI DOGS AND GOD'S GRACE

From the fullness of his grace we have all received one blessing after another. John 1:16

For you know the grace of our Lord Jesus Christ, that though he was rich, yet for your sakes he became poor, so that you through his poverty might become rich. 2 Corinthians 8:9

IT WAS AUGUST, 1956. School had started just a week ago, and the heat was remarkable. My new fourth grade teacher, Mrs. Ford had already told us there was no real person, living anywhere in the universe, whose name even slightly resembled Santa Clause or Saint Nicholas. There was a kid I had never seen who sat at the desk right behind me and was bigger than Mama's 32 year-old brother, my Uncle Dick. He had already shown me the coat hanger he was going to twist around my neck the first time I annoyed him. It was going to be a long year.

Some small sound woke me. Through my early sleepy morning mist I could hear them moving around and talking. The words weren't distinct, just the voices murmuring and the clink of dishes and sometimes a quiet laugh.

There was a muted creak of a screen door spring being

stretched open, and then the muffled thud as it banged shut.

I struggled between sleep and wakening. Somewhere I heard a lawnmower motor come reluctantly to life. I awoke just enough to realize something was different, then understood the difference with a rush of joy. This was Saturday. Today there would be no hateful school, no stiff scratchy blue jeans turned up six inches. No waiting for the bus, wondering if this would be the day the driver would completely ignore me, rolling by and leaving me standing, looking stupidly after the rear as the other kids laughed and pointed out the back window. Best of all, no fourth grade, and no Mrs. Ford.

My eyes jumped open. My sleepiness was gone. It was Saturday! The day stretched ahead. In my ten-year-old mind, Saturdays surely lasted thirty-six hours instead of twenty-four. This was Town Day. I was out of bed and into Friday's jeans (somewhat softer now with their two days of intensive wear) in an instant. Town Day! It was well worth five dreary days trapped in a school room with Mrs. Ford.

Mama was in the kitchen cleaning up from breakfast. "Run get your Daddy and tell him I got the store order ready."

"Where is he Mama?"

"Down in the garden I reckon; and tell him to bring some onions with him. Law, look at you, boy. You can't go to the store looking like that. You tell him, and then get back here and put on some clean britches. I've got some bacon left and I'll fix some eggs while you're gone."

They had been up a lot longer than I. I'd heard them in the kitchen. Mama always fixed the first meal of the day and they'd eat before it got good light. Our breakfast was usually bacon, fried eggs, perhaps sliced tomatoes or fried potatoes, toast and jelly.

The toast wasn't made in a pop-up toaster. Mama would put five or six slices of bread on a big cookie sheet, add a little square of butter right in the middle, and then sprinkle just a little less than a teaspoon of sugar over and around the butter. This was put on the top rack in the oven with the indicator turned to broil and toasted to a light golden brown. Even today, I can't abide toast made in a toaster. It seems that having both sides browned makes it too crunchy. When you think about it, even the word "toasty" better describes something lightly browned rather than hard and crunchy.

Oven toast has more character than pop-up toast too. Instead of plain brown crunchy squares of bread, when Mama's toast came out of the oven it would be golden tan with a big, round, yellow spot right in the middle. The melted sugar would make a shiny clear glaze right up to the edges. The big spot of yellow butter always reminded me of the morning sun.

I started to the garden knowing I would find Daddy hoeing or picking something before it got very hot. It wouldn't be long now before the corn, tomatoes and beans and other garden truck were all gone. In another six weeks it would start to get cooler at night, and not much longer after that we would have the first frost. Mama had been canning all summer, and the kitchen was decorated with long strings of green beans and hot peppers drying on heavy thread, hanging from little cup hooks Daddy had screwed into the ceiling.

I went down to the garden and found Daddy hoeing his four rows of Hickory King field corn. Daddy and almost everyone else I've ever heard, called it Hickory Cane. It wasn't until I moved away from home to Knoxville to attend the University of Tennessee, and read Chaucer's *Canterbury Tales* that I realized folks were actually saying "Hickory Kang." *Kang* was an East

Tennessee pronunciation of *King* that probably was a hold-over from our English Elizabethan ancestry. *Kang* likely then evolved to the logical *Cane*, corn being a cane plant; thus Hickory Cane.

He never planted the little yellow sweet corn. He claimed it didn't have much taste, so always grew the larger ears of white, which most folks usually grew for their livestock. It was delicious when pulled from the stalk, shucked and cleaned of the silk and the ears boiled "right then." Corn changes as it is absent from the stalk. The instant it is pulled, the natural sugar starts to convert to starch. The quicker you can get from the corn patch to the stove, the better your boiled ear of corn will taste. I know too, from experience, the more butter you can get to stick to an ear, the better it is.

He had already pulled the onions for dinner, the noon-time meal, and had picked a dish pan full of white half-runner green beans so Mama could put them on for supper. She would have to break and string them and have them on the stove with a big chunk of fatback bacon by one in the afternoon if they were to be ready by six in the evening. I took the beans and onions back to the kitchen and found my egg just ready.

Mama always liked lots of pepper on her egg. The fried egg on her plate went from creamy white (because she fried them in the bacon grease) with crinkly brown edges, to just plain black from about 3/4 teaspoon of McCormick pepper she sprinkled on it. I wondered if the inside of her mouth was the same as everybody else. I tried peppering mine once, and it seemed like it took most of the hide off. Water didn't help. I always watched her close to see if tears sprang up when she ate her eggs, but nothing unusual ever happened.

I ate, relishing the cholesterol and saturated fat that I would in later years learn to avoid. Being a devoted "sopper," even at that early age, I used the square of toast reserved specifically for that task, to get the very last bit of delicious yolk.

Mama finished cleaning up while I put on clean britches, and Daddy came in from the garden, bringing a Woodson's bag full of tomatoes. Sister Joy had gotten up by then. She had swept the kitchen and gotten dressed, and Mama had slipped us our half-dollar each weekly allowance. We loaded up and headed for that wonderful place: Town!

The main reason for making the Saturday trip was to do the weekly grocery shopping. Mama always made up her "store order" while Dad was in the garden, and Joy and I were waking up. I asked Mama once why she called her grocery list a store order.

Back when her father and my Dad worked in the coal mines, folks lived in company-owned houses. They received company-provided medical care and bought their food staples and groceries from the company-owned market.

Instead of receiving cash as wages, there would be a daily tally of the amount of coal each miner could load by hand into waiting box cars. It was then translated into a specified amount of pay per ton. They were then given credit at the company store, and could make purchases against the amount of credit recorded there. Mama remembers during the Great Depression (about 1933) her father loading perhaps 15-20 tons of coal daily and receiving about a dollar a day in wages.

The market was different from those we have today. All the merchandise was on shelves, but only employees had access to the goods. The miner's wife would walk up to a counter that separated the shelves and employees from the main front entrance. She would give the storekeeper a list on which was written items her family

71

needed. That list was called the store order. The storekeeper would look the list over, and make a mental estimate of the total purchase amount. He would then check his books to see if there had been sufficient coal loaded to cover what she needed. If her husband or son had loaded enough coal, he would then fill her order from his shelves.

A final tally was made at the end of each month. The coal mining company charged for housing, medical care, and even for coal used for heating and cooking. If any credit was still available, the family would receive the difference, not in cash, but in company script which could be spent only in the company establishment.

When arriving in LaFollette we always went in the back entrance of the WHITE STORE because there was more parking room. Parking spaces on the street in front of the store were always filled. Almost every family in the county came to town early Saturday morning and would spend the day, leaving as late evening approached and darkness started to fall.

I was always in a hurry to get from the front of the WHITE STORE down the sidewalk to what everyone called the dime store. The UNITED 5 & 10 CENT STORE was six doorways down the street. The businesses between failed to slow me very much, except for the poolroom.

We normally got to town before lunch, and there would always be a line of ladies blocking the sidewalk in front of The ROYAL LUNCH ROOM, our local poolhall. It would have been a scandal for a woman to go inside such a masculine establishment. The proprietor, however, made one concession to Southern female sensibilities. In honor of his locally famous dogs (a succulent creation of an OSCAR MAYER brand wiener on a KERNS bun with mustard, onion and a wonderful meaty chili) he had cut a window a foot wide and two feet high. The hungry ladies could form a line on the sidewalk and have their chili dogs handed through the window from inside. It would have been inhospitable to have done otherwise. To have withheld such a delight from any hungry human, and especially to withhold them from the fairer sex of LaFollette, Tennessee, would have been criminal.

The line that formed there, and the spicy smell of the cooking chili and fresh-cut onions always slowed me down. There was another obstacle in my headlong dash to see the unread Hardy Boy adventures and the new WALT DISNEY "Duck Books" at the UNITED 5 & 10 CENT STORE—the man on wheels. He had no legs, and moved about on a modified mechanic's creeper. Rolling noisily down the sidewalk, propelled by muscular arms and glove protected hands, he would set out his wares in front of Lawrence Rouse's SERVICE GROCERY. There were yellow and blue nickel pencils, feather dusters, and red, green and yellow-dyed rabbit's feet on chains. One thing always made me stop for a closer look; a little furry dog that barked and jumped when he was wound up and released. I always coveted one of those dogs, but was never able to save up enough to buy one.

Most of my hard-earned fifty cents per week allowance was spent on WALT DISNEY comic books and HARDY BOY mystery books. Joy, four years older and infinitely more sophisticated, followed at a more dignified and leisurely pace. It better suited her station in life, being fourteen. I don't know on what she spent her fifty cents but I suspect it was something feminine and useless, like hair ribbon, or scarfs.

One musical era, was nearing it's end, but another was poised to begin. Dean Martin's number one hit, *Memories Are Made Of This* was still being played on the local radio

73

station WLAF. There was also a new kid, Elvis Presley, from nearby Memphis, who had released a singularly peculiar song, *Hound Dog* that was being heard a lot too. Joy may have squandered some of her money on 45 RPM records. At that age, she was past the urge to buy the *Adventures of Nancy Drew,* the girl's counterpart to the *Hardy Boy Mysteries.*

The *Hardy Boy's Adventures*, by Frank Dixon, cost about 45 cents each for a hard bound book. It wasn't until years later, after graduating to Steinbeck and Faulkner, would I learn the author of the exploits of those stalwart chums, Frank Dixon, did not actually exist. He was not the stern but kind gentleman I imagined as I devoured those stories of friendship and adventure, but a ghostwriter paid by a businessman who provided authors with story outlines. An anonymous creator of various juvenile books would churn out about two volumes per month and be paid a flat rate of about $100 a book. I'm glad Mrs. Ford didn't have *that* information.

Daddy's gone now. We may not be especially sophisticated here in East Tennessee, but we are sure there is a heaven. That's where he is, and I'm pretty certain he's tending his garden and talking to his favorite Bible prophet, Isaiah.

Mama doesn't use pepper on her eggs anymore. In fact, the doctor told her to quit them and start on EGG BEATERS. Mama says you can't get enough pepper on a fake egg to do it any good, and she just gave up on eggs altogether.

Time has certainly passed, and as I am just starting to better understand the ways of the existence of man, I realize my fourth grade teacher was actually a kind and intelligent person. She must have been right, because in the 32 years since I weathered Mrs. Ford's fourth grade, I never once actually saw Saint Nicholas, though I believe I did hear him once.

In the New Testament, the twelfth chapter of 2 Corinthians, the Apostle Paul said he had a vision and saw into heaven. He wrote of elements of existence there we on earth couldn't yet comprehend, and God would not allow him to relate. I know what it was though. Our eternal existence does not begin when we die, but when we are able to solve that great mystery of living and come to realize our need for, and embrace, personally knowing our Creator. Part of heaven is being a ten-year-old boy, in 1956, Saturday morning, in town with a half-dollar in your pocket.

Solving the Great Mystery Of Life, by the way, is not a complex matter. Paul, in his letter to the Colossians, said his purpose in writing was that they might ". . . *know the mystery of God, namely Christ, in whom are hidden all the treasures of wisdom and knowledge.*" (Colossians 2:2b-3) Jesus Himself said it even more eloquently and unequivocally; *"I am the way and the truth and the life. No one comes to the Father except through Me."* (John 14:6)

Hot Dog Chili

1 Pound Ground Chuck
1 Large Chopped Onion
½ Teaspoon MEXENE Brand Chili Powder
½ Teaspoon Salt

In a large skillet, lightly brown the ground chuck and drain. Add the onion, chili powder and salt, and cook until the onion is soft.

═══════

Hot Dog Chili

½ Pound Ground Chuck
¼ Cup Water
1 Medium Chopped onion
1 Clove Garlic Or ⅛ Teaspoon Powdered Garlic
8 Ounces Tomato Sauce
½ Teaspoon MEXENE Brand Chili Powder
½ Teaspoon Salt

Brown the ground chuck and drain. Add water, onion, garlic, tomato sauce, chili powder and salt. Cook over medium heat for about twenty minutes, stirring occasionally.

Both these chili recipes are from Judy McLemore, a native of LaFollette, another devotee of Pool Room hot dogs. These are both close approximations of the original recipe, although not exact. In preparing this book I made a valiant effort to secure the original recipes, but unfortunately my polite requests to the establishment went unanswered.

The ROYAL LUNCH ROOM in LaFollette, Tennessee remains in operation, and if you ever have the opportunity, try one of their dogs. Similar creations may also be had at the WOODSON's DELI at WOODSON's MALL, and at Kenny Bartley's PIONEER TRADING POST on Middlesboro Highway East of LaFollette.

Every two weeks during both elementary school and high school our lunch was chili beans, slaw, cornbread and milk. As a matter of fact, the first paying commercial enterprise I engaged in was the sale of four bushels of sweet potatoes to the elementary school cafeteria. I rented garden space from our next-door neighbor and planted about a quarter acre of potatoes. The neighbor got one bushel and I sold the other four for $7.00 a bushel.

CHILI BEANS

2 Pounds Ground Chuck
2 Large Onions, Chopped
2 Rolls Chili Con Carne
   (12 Ounce Size)
6 Cans Pinto Beans,
   Without Pork (12 Ounce
   Size)
1½ Teaspoons Salt
½ Teaspoon Freshly Ground
   Black Pepper
1½ Teaspoons Chili Powder
1 Pint Water

In a large stock pot, brown the ground beef with the onions. Add the remaining ingredients and simmer for one hour. Yield: twelve servings.

CINNAMON TOAST

4 Slices White Bread
Butter
Sugar
Cinnamon

Place bread on a cookie sheet and in the center of each piece, put a thin pat of butter. Liberally sprinkle sugar and cinnamon over the butter and the entire surface of the bread. Place in the oven with the temperature set to broil. Toast very lightly. This may also be done with left-over biscuits split in half.

6 Pieces Bread, Cut Diagonally In Halves
2 Large Eggs
1 Cup Milk
2 Tablespoons Sugar
½ Teaspoon Nutmeg
1 Teaspoon Vanilla Flavoring
Shortening

Melt a little shortening in a large skillet. Mix the eggs, milk, sugar and cinnamon and beat well. Dip both sides of the bead into the mixture, place into the pan and brown both sides to golden. Serve with maple syrup, jelly or jam, or sprinkled with powdered sugar.

I have eaten gravy all over the South, and I suppose, generally speaking, the small diners of Atlanta make the best. The secret to making the best gravy is the meat you use. Any fried meat is okay, but sausage makes the best milk gravy. Sausage that is low in fat and does not have a lot of hot pepper and salt is the best choice. Of course, if the gravy is perfect and the biscuits are average, you have wasted your effort.

6 Tablespoons Meat Drippings (Use Bacon, Sausage, Chicken, Pork Chops Etc.)
8 Tablespoons Flour
2½ Cups Milk
Salt
Pepper

In a heavy ten-inch skillet in which you have fried chicken or some other meat, remove the drippings and return to the same skillet, six tablespoons of the fat. Heat to medium-high. Sprinkle the flour into the drippings and add about ¾ teaspoon salt and ⅛-¼ teaspoon of ground pepper to taste. Stir constantly and allow the roux to brown to a light caramel color. To achieve the best flavor, be sure to brown sufficiently; don't be too quick to add the milk. When flour is brown and smooth, add all the milk and continue stirring until the thickness is to your preference. The gravy will thicken slightly after being removed from the heat. Serve hot with biscuits and the fried chicken.

Fried Potatoes

8 Medium Potatoes
¼ Cup Oil
1 Teaspoon Salt

Peel and wash the potatoes. In a heavy skillet, heat the oil to medium. Dice the potatoes and add to the hot oil and cook uncovered for fifteen minutes, stirring and turning as necessary to prevent sticking. Reduce the heat to medium-low, cover and cook for an additional ten minutes, stirring once or twice. Remove the lid, salt to taste and cook another five-eight minutes until done.

When I told Mama I needed her recipe for fried potatoes, she thought I was kidding. "Why Ricky, everybody knows how to fry potatoes. They'll think you're addled if you put that in a book. You might as well put in a recipe for Boiled Eggs."

Mama is right most of the time, but about a week later, we were at The Fresh Market on Kingston Pike in Knoxville and I was looking through their cookbook display. I showed her a recipe for green beans. It said to string and break the beans, and then quickly cook them for 4 minutes so they would be sure to retain their crispness. Not everybody knows the basics. I decided someone might need the fried potato recipe.

80

The only variety of corn we used to eat was what Daddy called "Hickory Cane". I know now that this was one of two varieties called Hickory King or Hickory Queen.

Remember that as the corn sets after it is pulled, the natural sugar in it starts to turn to starch, causing it to lose its flavor. Boil it as soon as possible, never keeping it longer than a day.

BOILED CORN ON THE COB

8 Ears Of Fresh Corn,
  Just Picked
Water

Shuck the corn, remove the silks and cut off the ends. Cut the ears into manageable lengths and put them into a pot of boiling water. Continue boiling for 5 minutes, let set in the hot water for 3 more, and serve with plenty of butter and salt.

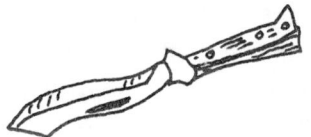

FRIED CORN

6-7 Ears Fresh Corn
½ Cup Butter Or Margarine
1-1½ Teaspoon Salt

Select corn that is full but still milky. Shuck the corn, remove any silks and cut off the ends. Hold an ear vertically in a shallow pan. Using a sharp knife and cutting from the top to the bottom, cut off the kernels. Be careful not to cut into the cob. When all the kernels have been removed, use the back (dull) side of your knife and scrape, extracting all the liquid or milk. Heat butter in a large cast-iron skillet, and add about ½ teaspoon salt to taste. If your butter or margarine is unsalted, use a bit more. Cook over medium heat, stirring frequently until thick, about eight-ten minutes. Mama adds from ¼-½ cup of evaporated milk if it starts to get too dry. Sometimes she adds just a pinch of sugar.

Corn is another of the foods that are native to America and not brought here by our ancestors from Europe.

I said this to someone and they pointed out that corn is mentioned in the Bible, which preceded the colonization of America. He was correct. The word appears 102 times in the King James Version of the Scriptures. That, however is an English transl-ation of Hebrew and Greek words, and they used the word "corn" in those times in Great Britain to refer to any kind of grain at all. So, when the Bible mentions corn, keep in mind that it is a reference to any kind of grain, and not our corn or Indian "maize."

CORN PUDDING

2 Cups Fresh Corn, Cut
  From Cob
1 Tablespoon Butter
2 Eggs, Whites And
  Yolks Separated
2 Cups Whole Milk
2 Tablespoons Flour
2-3 Tablespoons Sugar
Salt
Pepper, Freshly Ground

Cook the corn in a little water for about twenty minutes. Remove the cooked corn from the heat, and add milk, butter, salt, pepper, beaten egg yolks, flour and sugar. Beat the egg whites until stiff and fold them into the pudding mixture. Pour this into a buttered baking dish and bake at about 250 degrees for ½ hour. Serves five-six.

FRIED CORN CAKES

1-1½ Cups Cream Style
  Corn
1 Egg
¼ Cup Flour
¼ Cup Evaporated Milk
¼ Cup Oil

Heat the oil to medium in an iron skillet. Beat all the ingredients together and drop by tablespoons to about pancake-size in the hot oil. Turn and brown both sides to a light golden.

Corn Relish

12 Ears Fresh Corn
2 Large Onions, Chopped
2 Chopped Green Sweet Peppers
1 Chopped Red Bell Pepper (Or
   1 Small Jar Pimentos)
2 Cups Cabbage, Chopped
3 Tablespoons Salt
¼ Teaspoon Black Pepper
1 Tablespoon Dry Mustard or 2
   Tablespoons Prepared Mustard
2 Cups White Sugar
2 Cups Vinegar
1½ Tablespoons Celery Seed
½ Teaspoons Turmeric

Cut the corn from the cob, but do not scrape the cob. Add all the remaining ingredients and simmer slowly for one hour. Use the hot water bath canning method to preserve. Makes about 10-12 pints.

If you want a taste of what Heaven will be like, wait for a cold snowy December day, cook up a pot of pinto beans, a pone of cornbread, a skillet-full of fried potatoes, slice an onion and open a jar of corn relish; and then invite a good friend over for dinner.

You will have a better understanding of God's grace.

There are many things you can't eat unless there is a pone of cornbread nearby.

I ran across many cornbread recipes, and they were as varied as the cooks that presented them. I believe many people would fight over their cornbread recipe. There is even a debate whether it is correctly written "corn bread" or "cornbread." Some folks even add cheese and peppers to cornbread!

If it is to be good, it must have a heavy, rich brown crust, with the inside light but with a slightly coarse texture. To achieve this, you must bake it in a heavy cast-iron skill and use a hot oven, about 475º.

CORNBREAD

1¾ Cups Corn Meal Mix
1 Cup Buttermilk (Plus 1
    Tablespoon If Necessary)
2 Tablespoons Oil

Preheat the oven to 475 degrees. On the stove top over medium heat, in an eight-inch seasoned cast-iron skillet, heat the two tablespoons of oil. While the oil is heating, add the cornmeal mix to a mixing bowl. Gradually pour in the buttermilk as you stir. The resulting batter should not be thin, but should pour easily. Use additional buttermilk if necessary. When the oil is hot, quickly pour the cornbread batter into the skillet. The batter should sizzle and pop as it is poured in. Bake at 475 degrees for about 25 minutes or until the top begins to brown.

| 1 Cup Milk | 2 Cups Lukewarm Water |
| 4 Tablespoons Brown Sugar | 1 Teaspoon Salt |

4½ Cups Plus 2 Cups Sifted Wheat Flour
7 Tablespoons Fresh Corn Meal, Stone-Ground
3 Tablespoons Melted Shortening

Scald the milk and add 2 Tbsp. sugar, cornmeal and salt. Put the mixture into a loosely covered jar and place into a dish of water as hot as the hand can bear. Keep it in a warm place overnight. You may even set this over the pilot light on a gas stove, or near the wood stove if it is wintertime. By morning the mixture should show fermentation and gas can be heard to escape. Add 2 cups of sifted wheat flour, 2 cups lukewarm water, 2 tablespoons brown sugar and 3 tablespoons of melted shortening. Beat this mixture thoroughly. Place it again into a dish of warm water and let rise until light and full of bubbles, then add about 4½ cups sifted wheat flour or enough to make a stiff dough. Knead for 10-15 minutes, then mold into loaves. Place the dough into greased pans and let rise again until light. Bake for 15 minutes at 425° and then lower temperature to 375 and bake 30 minutes longer.

This makes lovely, wonderfully textured loaves and has never failed. This bread has no yeast and relies on the salt-tolerance of the cornmeal for fermentation. You will be better guaranteed success if you use very fresh meal from a stone mill.

An excellent place to obtain fresh corn meal in the East Tennessee area is at the OLD MILL in Pigeon Forge, near Gatlinburg. The mill is just about a block off the main four-lane highway, on the left side, about half way through town, as you go toward Gatlinburg. Ask any merchant for directions.

POTATO CAKES

5 Medium Potatoes,
  Peeled and Grated
2 Tablespoons Flour
1 Teaspoon Salt
1 Tablespoon Grated
  Onion
1 Egg, Well Beaten
2-3 Tablespoons Oil
Dash Garlic Salt
  (Optional)

Place the grated potatoes in a saucepan, cover with cold water and drain. Do this three times. Add all the other ingredients, except the oil, to the drained potatoes and mix well. Heat the oil to medium in a cast-iron skillet and using about ¼ cup of the mixture to form each cake, brown the cakes to golden on each side. Serve with commercial sour cream or applesauce to spread on the cakes, or serve in the place of bread with any meal, especially pork.

RAW POTATO PANCAKES

2 Medium Sized Grated
  Raw Potatoes
2 Egg Yolks, Beaten
1 Tablespoon Salt
½ Teaspoon Baking
  Powder
1 Tablespoon Sugar
2 Heaping Tablespoons
  Flour
2 Egg Yolks, Beaten

Place the raw potatoes in a clean cloth and remove any water by squeezing. Add salt, baking powder, sugar and flour. Mix thoroughly, add the egg whites, mix again, and proceed as with pancakes. This recipe makes about 10 Potato Pancakes, and may be doubled.

FRESH GREEN BEANS WITH PORK

Approximately ½ Gallon
Freshly Picked
Green Beans
3-4 Inch Portion Cured,
Peppered Side Meat
2-3 Teaspoons Salt

Put washed, stringed and broken beans into a kettle, cover with water (about one quart) and add meat which has been scored and cut into two or three pieces. Cover the kettle and bring to a boil. Reduce the heat to low-medium and cook, covered, approximately 3½-4 hours. Check occasionally and add water, about ½ cup at a time, to keep from sticking.

After cooking for about 2½-3 hours, or until beans are tender, taste and add salt (if necessary) to taste. Uncover and cook until the liquid is reduced to about ¼-½ cup.

If less time is available, you may reduce the heat to only medium instead of low and cook for a shorter time, about 2½ hours. Check and adjust the seasoning at about two hours, and then cook uncovered to reduce the liquid.

To use home-canned beans instead of fresh, substitute 2 quarts canned for the ½ gallon of fresh and follow the same recipe except for the following changes. Use the canned beans and their liquid. Cover the kettle and bring to a boil, reduce the heat to low-medium and cook, covered, approximately one hour. As with the fresh, check occasionally and add water to keep from sticking. After cooking for an hour, add salt to taste. Uncover and continue to cook until the liquid is reduced to about ¼-½ cup.

Serve with cornbread, sliced tomatoes, sliced onions and pot roast.

"Some folks call 'em shuck beans, and some call 'em leather britches, I guess 'cause they're so wrinkled and tough looking. You just get you about a half bushel of white half runners and break 'em up like you're going to cook 'em, except you string 'em up on heavy string with a great big needle. Then you hang 'em up in a dry airy place for about two weeks. When they're done, you can put 'em in a bag in the freezer."

½ Gallon Dried Green Beans
Ham Hock Or ½ Pound
    Peppered Side Meat
½-¾ Teaspoon Salt

Remove the dried green beans from the yarn they were dried on. Place them in a large kettle, cover with water and let soak overnight. The next morning, drain and rinse the beans well. Cover again with water and cook covered on low heat for about three hours. Add a large country ham hock or about ¾ pound peppered side meat and cook another three hours, covered. Remove the cover, add salt to taste and cook another 20-30 minutes until almost all the liquid is gone. Serve with cornbread, fried potatoes, fried hog jowl, sliced onions, molasses, and pickled beets.

CREAMED NEW POTATOES

1 Quart New Potatoes
3 Tablespoons Bacon Drippings
  Or ½ Stick Butter
2 Heaping Tablespoons Flour
1 Small Can Evaporated Milk
  (6 Ounce)
½ Teaspoon Salt
Freshly Ground Black Pepper

Wash and scrub the skin from the potatoes, cutting them in half if they are as large as an egg. In a saucepan, cover them with water and season with the bacon drippings or butter. Cook for about twenty minutes or until tender, making sure that when finished cooking, there is still enough liquid to cover the potatoes. If the liquid cooks away, add a little water. When the potatoes are almost done, beat the flour and the evaporated milk until smooth, slowly add to the potatoes, and stirring constantly, cook until thick and creamy. Sprinkle with black pepper.

Prepare this meal as a spring tonic. Fix up a bowl of poke and scrambled eggs, pull some tiny green onions, make some corn-bread, and open a jar of pickled beets.

NEW POTATOES WITH PEAS

1 Quart New Potatoes,
  Whole And Scraped
2 Cups Freshly Shelled
  Garden Peas
½ Stick Butter
¼ Teaspoon Pepper
¾ Teaspoon Salt

Place all the ingredients in a saucepan, add one cup of water, cover tightly and cook until tender. Check occasionally and add water if it begins to cook away.

CREAMED GREEN PEAS

2 Cups Freshly Shelled
  Green Peas
1 Teaspoon Salt
½ Cup Heavy Cream

Cook the shelled green peas quickly in boiling water until tender. Add one level teaspoon salt, stir well, then drain off the water and add the ½ cup of cream. Slowly bring to a boil, allow to thicken and serve hot.

Okra Soup

1 Soup Bone, Cracked
4 Cups Water
4 Cups Fresh Okra, Sliced
   Crossways
2 Cups Skinned Tomatoes
1 Teaspoon Salt
½ Teaspoon Black Pepper

Cover the soup bone with water and bring to a boil. Reduce the heat, cover and cook for one hour. To the broth add the okra and tomatoes (canned tomatoes may be substituted). Simmer uncovered for 2 hours, or until thick. Serve with rice and boiled corn on-the-cob. Be sure to pick small to medium sized okra; if it is large it becomes tough.

For years the only way I would eat okra was very crisply fried. When stewed, okra presents a patently unsavory appearance. This is not the case with this soup, however. The gluey sap that has given okra its infamous reputation acts as a thickening agent and makes this dish "gumbo-like."

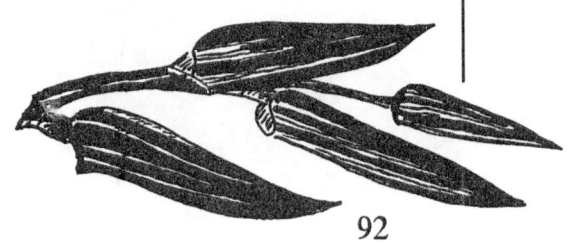

92

Mama is the only one in our family that likes butter or lima beans. They have a bland flavor to me, but I guess if you put enough ham hock or salt pork in anything it will end up tasting pretty good.

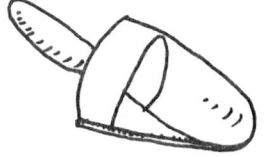

BUTTER BEANS

3-4 Cups Dried Butter Beans
   (Limas)
Salt Pork Or Other
   Seasoning Pork
Salt

Do not soak the beans as you would pintos. Wash and "look" the beans, place them in a pot, cover with water and bring to a boil. Drain the water, cover the beans again with water and add the scored salt pork. Return to a boil, reduce heat, cover and cook for about 2½ hours at medium-low. When the beans are tender, taste and add salt as necessary. Do not salt until the beans have finished cooking. Adding salt at the beginning of the cooking process will cause the beans to be hard.

MASHED POTATOES

8 Medium Potatoes
¼ Cup Whole Milk
5 Tablespoons Butter
Salt
Pepper

There is a *Beth Doctrine*. It states, "Never serve mashed potatoes without peas and gravy."

Peel the potatoes and dice, then cover with water and bring to a boil. Reduce the heat and cook until the potatoes are tender. Drain the water, add butter and some of the milk and mash with a potato masher. Add the rest of the milk a little at-a-time until the potatoes reach the correct texture. Taste and add salt and pepper as necessary. Place in a serving dish, add a large pat of butter to the top as a garnish and serve hot.

BAKED ZUCCHINI WITH TOMATOES

3 Medium Zucchini
(About ¾
Pound)
3 Ripe Medium
Tomatoes
1 Medium Green
Pepper
½ Cup Chopped
Onions
2½ Teaspoons
Finely Chopped
Garlic
2 Teaspoons Dried
Marjoram
1 Teaspoon
Oregano
Ground Black
Pepper
1 Teaspoon Salt
2½ Tablespoons
Olive Oil
2 Tablespoons
Freshly Grated
Parmesan
Cheese

Preheat the oven to 425 degrees. Cut off the stem and blossom ends of the zucchini and core the tomatoes. Cut the zucchini and tomatoes crosswise into slices. Arrange the zucchini and tomato slices in a baking dish with the edges slightly overlapping. Alternate layers of zucchini and tomatoes. Core, seed and chop the green pepper. Put the chopped green pepper, onions, garlic and marjoram into a mixing bowl and add ground pepper and salt to taste. Blend well, and scatter the mixture over the layered tomatoes and zucchini. Sprinkle with olive oil and cheese. Bake for 20-25 minutes until just lightly browned. Yield: four servings.

This is a wonderful dish, and one of my favorites. Be sure to try it. These little crookneck yellow squash are really easy to grow too; you just put them into the ground and step back. Warn your neighbors, though, because they will find bags full from an anonymous donor all summer long.

To prepare the squash, wash them, cut off ends, slice into a saucepan, cover with water, bring to a boil and cook until tender, about ten minutes. Drain and mash. It is unnecessary to peel the squash unless they are large and the skin has become tough.

Combine the mayonnaise, onion, ¼ cup cracker crumbs, egg, sugar, salt and pepper. Add the mashed squash and mix well. Pour the blend into a lightly greased one quart casserole. Sprinkle all the remaining cracker crumbs over the squash mixture. Bake uncovered at 350 degrees for 25-30 minutes. Sprinkle cheese on top, and bake an additional five minutes until the cheese melts. This recipe will yield about four servings, or two if the meal is for one other person and me.

BAKED SUMMER SQUASH

¼ Cup Mayonnaise
½ Cup Onion
½ Cup Cracker Crumbs, Divided
1 Egg, Beaten
1 Teaspoon Sugar
¼ Teaspoon Salt
⅛ Teaspoon Ground Pepper
1 Pound Yellow Squash, About 5 Cleaned, Boiled and Mashed
⅛ Cup Shredded Sharp Cheddar Cheese

SQUASH PIE

This is a pie that is not very sweet, but is very good when accompanied by freshly brewed coffee.
Use any summer squash for this dessert, although yellow crookneck is best.

2 Cups Squash
¾ Teaspoon Ginger
½ Teaspoon Cinnamon
3 Eggs, Slightly Beaten
1½ Cups Half & Half
½ Teaspoon Nutmeg
Pinch Salt
Honey
½ Cup Chopped Nuts
Unbaked Pie Shell

Rub the squash through a sieve. With the squash, combine the spices, eggs, cream, and salt, mixing well. Pour the blend into an unbaked pie shell. Bake in a 425 degree oven for about 25 minutes or until an inserted knife comes out clean. Cool and cover with honey and finely chopped nuts.

White Beans

1 Pound Dried Great Northern
   Beans
2 x 2-Inch Piece Of Peppered
   Side Meat
1 Teaspoon Salt (Or To Taste)

Pick over the dried beans to remove any gravel and bad beans. Wash thoroughly twice and drain. Cover with cold water and add the seasoning meat, scored but not cut through. Cover and bring to a boil then reduce the heat to medium-low. Cook covered until tender (about three hours). When the cooking time is almost done, add a teaspoon of salt and freshly ground black pepper to taste. Serve with cornbread and pickle relish.

Don't confuse these with Navy Beans or Pea Beans, both of which need to be soaked before cooking.

Did you know there are more than 25 varieties of dried beans available? They include black, turtle, kidney black-eyed, pintos chick-peas, etc.

One cup of dried beans will produce 2½ cups of cooked beans. One cup of dried beans will provide you with 60% of your daily protein need, 65% of the iron, and 4.3 grams of dietary fiber.

Most of the apples produced in the U.S. are from Michigan, Washington and New York. About half are eaten as fresh fruit and the other half is commercially canned as sauce or pie filling, or the juice made into cider, vinegar, drinking juice or jelly. In Europe, most of the juice is made into brandy or wine.

Some of the best apples and cider I have ever had, though, came from Cosby, Tennessee. There are several orchards between Newport and Cosby on Cosby Highway. From Gatlinburg, ask somebody how to get to Cosby, and when you get there, head toward Newport, keeping your eyes open.

SPICED APPLE SAUCE

6-8 Winesap Apples
1 Cup Sugar (More If Desired)
½ Teaspoon Cinnamon
¼ Teaspoon Ground Cloves
¼ Teaspoon Allspice
½ Cup Water

Wash, peel and quarter the apples into a saucepan. Add about ½ cup water and one cup of sugar. Cook the apples until they are soft. Depending on the type of apples used, this will take from fifteen-thirty minutes. Using a potato masher, crush until the apples are smooth and free of lumps. Add cinnamon, cloves and allspice. Continue to cook until the applesauce reaches the desired texture. Serve as a side dish with pork, or as an accompaniment to spice cake.

99

25-30 Medium Sized Cucumbers
8 Large White Onions
3 Large Sweet Peppers
½ Cup Salt
5 Cups Apple Cider Vinegar
2 Tablespoons Mustard Seed
1 Teaspoon Tumeric
½ Teaspoon Ground Cloves

Here is a fine sandwich. Use sourdough bread, mayonnaise, these bread and butter pickles, and braunschweiger.

You will need to hide somewhere to eat it, for if anyone sees it you will have to share.

Wash the cucumbers and slice very thin. Slice the onions and chop peppers; combine with the cucumbers and blend salt into the mixture. Cover with a clean cloth and let stand for 3 hours. Drain the liquid from the vegetable mixture. Combine the vinegar, sugar and spices in a large kettle. Bring to a boil and add the vegetable mixture. Heat thoroughly, until boiling (but do not boil). While hot, pack the pickles into sterilized jars, leaving ½-inch head space. Remove any air bubbles by running a table knife around the inside of the jars, and wipe the rims. Cover at once with metal lids, and screw on metal bands. Process the jars in a boiling water bath for 10 minutes to seal.

Mama and Pat still fix this occasionally, but Daddy wouldn't hardly eat it. He said that it was about all they fixed when he was in the Army, and they "burnt him out on it."

1 Jar ARMOUR Sliced Dried Beef
   (2¼ Ounce)
3 Tablespoons Oil, Or Butter
1½ Cups Evaporated Milk
1½ Cups Water
6 Tablespoons Flour
¼-½ Teaspoons Salt
¼ Teaspoon Pepper
Dash Worcestershire Sauce
   (Optional)
6-8 Slices White Bread, Toasted

Rinse the dried beef in warm water for fifteen seconds and drain. Cut or tear into smaller pieces and add to hot oil in a medium sized skillet. Cook until lightly browned and remove from the skillet with a slotted spoon. Add enough oil or butter to the skillet to return the amount to three tablespoons. Add flour to the hot fat in the skillet and stir until it turns light brown. Mix together the evaporated milk and water and add to the skillet. Stirring constantly, cook until thick. Return the beef to the skillet, add salt and pepper to taste and Worcester sauce if desired. Mix well and heat through. Serve over toast.

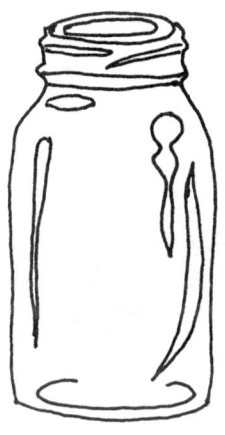

101

6-8 Medium Cut Pork Chops
1 Cup Uncooked Rice
6 Beef Bouillon Cubes
8 Slices Onions
8 Slices Bell Pepper
8 Slices Tomato
¼ Cup Cooking Oil
3 Cups Water, Boiling

In very large skillet (Mama uses an electric skillet) brown the chops in hot oil on both sides. Remove the pork chops from the pan, scrape the bottom to loosen any bits of meat, and very carefully (for it will steam and splash) add three cups of boiling water to the drippings in the pan. Add the bullion cubes and stir until they are dissolved. You may want to put just a bit of very hot water in a cup and have the bouillon already dissolved. Add the rice, and then arrange the chops on top of the rice. Place, in this order, a slice of onion, pepper and tomato on each chop. Cover and simmer until the chops are tender and the liquid is absorbed, about an hour and fifteen minutes. More water may be added during cooking if needed.

The cultivation of rice began about five thousand years ago in China. If you, like I, disagree with the evolutionary theory of creation, that was not long after God brought man to this planet.

It was introduced to Europe through Italy in the 1400's, and eventually found its way to England, where it was carried to our shores by the American colonists. It was successfully cultivated in South Carolina in the early 1600's and from there became a major food staple in the South.

I found this recipe in Wilson Hain's, "Grandmother Pete's" recipe box. She worked in some capacity with the White House in the 1950's or 6-0's. A note at the bottom of the index card on which it was written said, "Ike's Favorite."

Sirloin Steak, About 1½-Inch Thick
¼ Cup Butter
1 Tablespoon Worcestershire Sauce
1 Teaspoon Garlic Powder
1 Teaspoon Salt
Dash Pepper

Preheat the oven for five minutes on broil. Melt the butter and stir in Worcestershire sauce, garlic powder, salt and pepper. Place the steak on a rack in a foil-lined pan and brush generously with the butter sauce.

Broil three inches from the broiling unit for seven-eight minutes. Turn the steak by poking a fork in the fat part, brush with more butter sauce and broil seven-eight minutes on the second side. This is for rare steak. For medium-rare steak, broil for nine-ten minutes. If your steak is not quiet 1½-inches thick, you must reduce the cooking time.

Transfer the steak to a warm serving platter and pour the remaining sauce over the browned beef.

Pot Roast

3-5 Pound Pork Or Beef Roast
¼ Cup Oil
¼ Teaspoon Accent
¼ Teaspoon Garlic Powder
½ Teaspoon Salt
¼ Teaspoon Freshly Ground
    Pepper
6-8 Potatoes, Peeled And
    Quartered
3-4 Carrots, Peeled And Sliced
3 Medium Onions, Quartered

Rub the seasonings into the meat. In a large pot, heat the oil to medium and then add the roast. Brown the roast on all sides. Add enough hot water to cover the meat half way. Reduce the heat, cover, and simmer until tender, about 2 hours, depending on the size of the roast. Remove the meat to a baking dish and put into a 350° oven until crisp and brown. To the broth in the pot, add potatoes, onions, and carrots. Add enough hot water to cover the vegetables if necessary. Cook covered, on medium until they are tender, about 30 minutes. Add salt and pepper to taste, but remember that salt was added to the roast when it was cooking.

When the vegetables have finished cooking, serve them in their broth. If desired, the broth may be thickened slightly by adding ¼ cup cornstarch to ½ cup cold water and then adding this mixture to the broth and cooking for an additional three-four minutes.

104

Apple Jelly

5 Pounds Apples (For 7 Cups Juice)   9 Cups Sugar
1 Package Fruit Pectin (¾ Ounce)   5 Cups Water
                    ½ Teaspoon Butter

Wash the apples, remove stems, cut off blossom ends, and cut into quarters. It is unnecessary to peel or core the apples. Place in a large pot. Add five cups of water and bring to a boil. Reduce the heat, cover and simmer for ten minutes. Remove from the heat and use a potato masher to crush the cooked apples. Cover and simmer for five minutes longer. Stir the apples occasionally during the cooking time.

Pour the cooked apple pulp into a jelly bag in a large bowl. If you have no bag, improvise one from three layers of damp cheesecloth. Tie the bag closed, hang and let it drip into a container until the dripping stops. Press gently to remove any remaining juice from the pulp. Measure the juice, and if you have too little, you may add up to ½ cup water to bring to an accurate measurement.

Prepare glass jars by boiling them in a large pot filled with water, for ten minutes. Leave the jars in the hot water until ready to fill.

In a pan, to exactly seven cups of juice, add the 1¾ ounce package of fruit pectin, and ½ teaspoon butter. Bring to a boil over high heat, stirring constantly. Add exactly nine level cups of sugar to the mixture, allow to return to a full boil, and continue boiling for one minute, stirring constantly. Remove the mixture from the stove and skim any foam from the surface.

Fill the jars to about ¼-inch of the top. Wipe the rims and cover with a ⅛-inch thick layer of melted paraffine. Yield: ten cups of apple jelly.

The addition of the butter will decrease foam on the juice. The paraffine should be as near ⅛-inch as possible. Thicker is not better.

4 Cups Capped, Washed
Strawberries
(Including Some
Underripe Ones)
1 Tablespoon Vinegar
3 Cups Sugar

Put the berries into a heavy pan, add vinegar, bring to a boil and then cover and boil for one minute. Add three cups of sugar and boil gently, uncovered, for twenty minutes, stirring occasionally. Pour the hot berries into a bowl and let stand, covered with a clean cloth overnight. They will look very liquid, but the berries plump up and absorb the syrup as they stand. The next morning, ladle the cold fruit into sterilized jars and cover immediately with ⅛-inch of melted paraffin. This will make five-six, five ounce glasses of preserves.

One of the prettiest sights I can recall was during the blizzard of '93. We had the dining room blinds raised so we could watch the snow. Twelve to fourteen inches were already on the ground and huge puffy flakes were falling straight down. The shrubs outside the window were bent with the weight of the snow and a cardinal and his mate were pecking around trying to dislodge the little berries that were not covered by the snow. Pat had put by some strawberry preserves the previous summer and had them sitting on the old oak pie safe beside the window. I happened to walk by and caught the perfect picture of the snow and a bright red cardinal framed by the window, complimented by the sparkling red of the strawberries in the glass jars on the safe.

106

3 Eggs, Separated	2¼ Teaspoons Baking Powder
1½ Cups Sugar	½ Teaspoon Salt
¾ Cups Butter	½ Cup Milk
½ Teaspoon Vanilla Flavoring	1 Large Fresh Coconut
2¼ Cups Plain Flour	½ Cup Coconut Milk

Reserve ½ cup of the coconut milk and mix with ½ cup whole milk to be used later. Beat the egg whites until they form peaks. Continue beating, gradually adding ½ cup sugar, and then set aside. Cream the butter with the vanilla and remaining sugar and then blend in the egg yolks. In another bowl, sift together flour, salt and baking powder. To the butter mixture, alternately add flour and the reserved coconut-whole milk mixture and finish by blending. Grate ¼ cup of the coconut flesh into the above mixture. Into this fold the egg whites. Using either a tube pan or three, eight-inch pans, greased and floured, bake in a 350° oven for 25-30 minutes or until done. While the cake is cooling, make the frosting.

Frosting

2 Egg Whites	¾ Cup Sugar
¼ Cup Water	1 Teaspoon Vanilla Flavoring
⅓ Cup Light Corn Syrup	⅛ Teaspoon Cream Of Tarter

Beat the egg whites until stiff and set aside. Mix sugar, corn syrup and water and cook covered at medium heat for about 3 minutes. Uncover and cook until mixture will "spin a thread" (238-240° on a candy thermometer). Whip the egg whites until frothy and to them add the syrup in a very thin stream, whipping constantly. When these ingredients are all combined, add cream of tarter and vanilla. Frost the cake when it has cooled. Garnish with some of the grated fresh coconut.

CHERRY COBBLER

Crust For Cobblers

2 Cups Plain Flour   ⅓ Cup Shortening
1 Teaspoon Salt   ¾ Cup Whole Milk
        1 Tablespoon Baking Powder

Sift together the dry ingredients and using a fork or pastry blender, cut the shortening into the mixture until it resembles coarse cornmeal. Add the milk and further blend the mixture into a light dough. Turn the dough onto a floured surface and knead until smooth. Roll out very thin. Line an 8 x 8-inch baking dish with the dough, reserving enough to make the top after the filling has been added.

The Filling

4 Cups Cherries   1 Cup Sugar
        4 Tablespoons Butter

Prepare and pit the cherries and mix them with the sugar. Bring the cherries and sugar to a boil and pour the mixture into the pie crust. Cut the butter into small pieces on top of the cherries. Using the dough reserved from the crust, roll out and cut it into one-inch wide strips. Arrange these strips on top of the fruit in a lattice pattern. Bake in a 350 degree oven until brown, usually about 45 minutes.

This dish was born of the necessity of waste not, want, not. It is a tasty way to use up stale, left-over biscuits, etc.

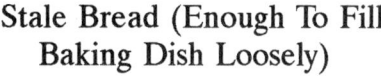

Stale Bread (Enough To Fill
  Baking Dish Loosely)
3 Eggs
1 Cup Sugar
2 Cups Whole Milk
½ Cup Raisins
½ Cup Coconut
1 Tablespoon Vanilla
Nutmeg

Break the bread in small pieces and place them into a baking dish. Beat the eggs, adding sugar. Beat in the milk and add the vanilla. Stir in the raisins and coconut. Pour this mixture over the bread and press with the back of a large spoon. If there isn't enough liquid, add a little more milk. Sprinkle liberally with freshly ground nutmeg. Let stand 45 minutes to one hour. Bake in a 350 degree oven for about one hour until lightly browned. Serve hot with vanilla ice-cream.

BANANA PUDDING

5 Ripe Bananas
6 Eggs, Separated
4 Cups Milk
1½ Cups Sugar
4 Tablespoons Flour
1 Tablespoon Plus 1 Teaspoon
    Vanilla Flavoring
Vanilla Wafers

Reserve the egg whites for the meringue. Stir all but ¼ cup of the sugar with the 4 Tbsp. flour. Beat in the egg yolks until well blended. Stir in the milk and cook in a double boiler over medium heat until the mixture boils and thickens. Add the vanilla. Remove from the heat and set aside to cool. While cooling, peel and slice crosswise, 5 ripe bananas. In the bottom of a 2-quart baking dish, place a layer of vanilla wafers. Cover the wafers with a layer of banana slices. Spread over them, a layer of the warm pudding. Repeat this process until the dish is full. Beat the egg whites until frothy and add a pinch of cream of tarter plus the reserved ¼ cup sugar, and beat until stiff peaks form. When the meringue is stiff, but before it becomes dry, spread it over the top of the pudding, being sure to seal the edges. Bake in a preheated 350 degree oven for about fifteen minutes or until the meringue is lightly browned. Serve at room temperature.

Then God said, "I give you every seed-bearing plant on the face of the whole earth and every tree that has fruit with seed in it. They will be yours for food. And to all the beasts of the earth and all the birds of the air and all the creatures that move on the ground—everything that has the breath of life in it—I give every green plant for food." And it was so. Genesis 1:29-30

LEMON MERINGUE PIE

1 Cup + 3 Tbsp. Sugar	1 Tsp. Grated Lemon Rind
3 Tbsp. Corn Starch	¼ Tsp.Cream Of Tarter
3 Egg Yolks	Cold Water
3 Egg Whites	Baked Pie Crust
¼ Cup Fresh Lemon Juice	½ Cup Powdered Sugar
1 Teaspoon Vanilla Flavoring	

This pie filling is translucent and not milky. Daddy called it "Nose Pie" because Mama made the meringue topping *high*, and if you were not careful when eating, it might get on your nose.

Mix one cup plus three tablespoons sugar with three tablespoons corn starch. Add ¼ cup cold tap water to make a thick paste. Add three egg yolks (save the whites, but don't refrigerate). Beat the yolks with a wire whisk until well mixed. Add the fresh lemon juice, lemon rind and an additional one cup water. Cook in a double boiler over medium heat until thick. I asked Mama, "how thick," and she said to cook it until the time you can take some up with a spoon and it just "plops" when you drop it back into the pan. That means *real thick*. It works out to about 20-30 minutes of cooking. Pour the filling into a baked pie shell. Beat the reserved egg whites until they become foamy, then add the cream of tarter and teaspoon vanilla. Add ½ cup powdered sugar, one tablespoon at-a-time. After all the sugar has been added, continue beating until the meringue will form a stiff peak. Spoon the meringue onto the Lemon Pie. Sprinkle with about ¼-½ teaspoon of granulated sugar. Brown for about fifteen minutes in a preheated, 350 degree oven or until just brown. Leave the oven door cracked just a bit, and watch closely, as the meringue burns easily. Be careful of your nose.

PEACH COBBLER

1 Stick Butter	1 Teaspoon Vanilla Extract
1 Cup Flour	¼ Tsp. Freshly Grated Nutmeg
1½ Tsp. Baking Powder	¼ Teaspoon Salt
¾ Cup Milk	2 Cans Sliced Peaches

1 Cup Sugar, Separated Into ¾ And ¼ Cup

Place butter in a baking dish and melt in a 350° oven. Prepare the batter by sifting together the flour, baking powder, salt and 1 cup sugar. Add the milk and beat. Add the vanilla and nutmeg and blend. Remove the butter from the oven, pour the batter over it and using a slotted spoon, add the peaches. Pour the peach juice over everything and sprinkle ¼ cup sugar over the top. Finally, grate a bit of nutmeg over the surface. Bake at 350° for about 45 minutes. The crust will rise to the top as the cobbler bakes.

PEACH PIE

3 Cups Fresh Or Sliced Peaches	½ Cup Sugar
1 Tablespoon Lemon Juice	⅛ Teaspoon Salt
3 Tablespoons Cornstarch	2 Teaspoons Butter
½ Teaspoon Almond Extract	Baked Pie Shell

Peel and slice the peaches, add 1 tablespoon lemon juice, sprinkle the sugar over the peaches, cover and let stand 1-2 hours. Drain the juice and reserve. Add corn starch to the juice and cook over low heat, stirring, until thick. Remove from the stove, add butter, salt and almond flavoring. Allow to cool and mix with the peaches. Pour the mixture into a baked pie shell. Cool and serve with ice-cream.

GRANDMOTHER HAIN'S
BEST NUT BREAD

Grandmother Hain was Wilson Hain's great grandmother. He was kind enough to let me use his Grandmother "Pete's" recipe box, in which I found this Nut Bread.

2½ Cups Sifted Flour
3½ Teaspoons Baking Powder
¾ Cups Sugar
½ Teaspoons Salt
1 Egg, Beaten
1½ Cups Milk
2 Tablespoons Melted Butter
½ Teaspoon Cinnamon
½ Cup Chopped Raisins (Optional)
¾ Cup Coarsely Chopped Nuts

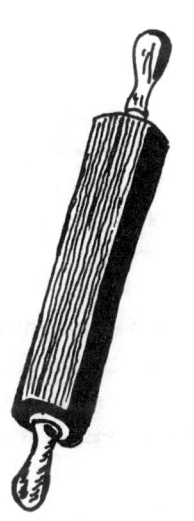

Sift together the flour, sugar, baking powder and salt. In a separate container, combine the beaten egg, milk, butter and cinnamon. Add this last mixture to the dry ingredients and mix well. Stir in the nuts and raisins and pour into a greased loaf pan.

Here is the trick in baking this dish: do not preheat the oven. Place the loaf into a cold oven, then turn the oven to 350°. Bake for about one hour. When done, remove the Nut Bread from the pan and cool on a rack. Store in an air-tight container or wrap in foil. If the raisins are omitted, add an additional ¼ cup nuts.

113

JAMBALAYA

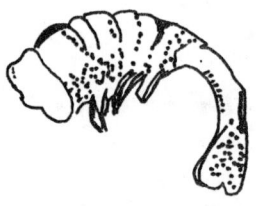

1 Pound Raw Shrimp, Cleaned
   And Deveined
½ Pound Bacon, Diced
1½ Cups Canned Tomatoes
2 Cups Water
¾ Cup Onion, Chopped
1 Cup Green Pepper, Chopped
1 Clove Garlic, Minced
2 Tablespoons Minced Parsley
1 Tablespoon Salt
¼ Teaspoon Freshly
   Ground Black Pepper
½ Teaspoon Thyme
⅛ Teaspoon Tabasco Sauce
1 Teaspoon Worcestershire Sauce
1 Cup Uncooked Rice (Not
   Instant)

Partially fry the bacon in a dutch oven. Drain off the excess fat, add shrimp and tomatoes, and simmer for about six minutes. Add and stir in water, onions, green pepper, garlic, parsley and seasonings. Bring to a boil, lower heat, cover and simmer for about twelve minutes. Stir in the rice, replace the lid and simmer for twenty minutes more, or until the rice is tender. This makes about six, one-cup servings.

No one knows for sure where the name came from, but Jambalaya itself has been a favorite in Louisiana since old Creole times. Although not an original Appalachian recipe, it is a modern adaptation and simplifies the procedure while preserving the delicious combinations of flavors that generations of Southerners have learned to love.

114

PAN FRIED FISH

2 Pounds Fish Fillets
1 Cup Corn Meal
½ Cup Flour
1¼ Teaspoons Black Pepper
Pinch Cayenne Pepper
½ Teaspoon Paprika
2 Teaspoons Salt
1½ Cup Buttermilk
Shortening or Lard

This is best fixed on the lake while on a camping trip, accompanied by hush puppies, fried potatoes and strong, black coffee.

Catfish, bass, trout, or almost any fresh fish fillets are good for this recipe. In a heavy cast-iron skillet, melt enough shortening to make about ¼-inch. Mix the dry ingredients. Place the fish in a large bowl and pour the buttermilk over the fillets and allow them to set at room temperature for about ten minutes. Remove the fish from the buttermilk and dip both sides in the dry ingredients. Fry in shortening over medium-high heat for about three minutes to a side. Serve with french-fried potatoes, hush puppies and coleslaw.

115

HUSH PUPPIES

2 Cups Plain Corn Meal
1 Cup Plain Flour
2 Teaspoons Soda
¾ Teaspoon Salt
1 Cup Buttermilk (Approximate)
1 Large Chopped Onion

Pan fry the fish, and use the oil that remains to fry your hush puppies. Mix all the dry ingredients and then add buttermilk, a little at-a-time to make a stiff batter. Add the chopped onion and stir. Spoon the batter so that it resembles small (about 2½-inch) pancakes into the hot fat in a heavy skillet. Fry until brown, turn and fry the other side and drain on paper towels. Serve hot with fish and french-fries or fried potatoes.

A tasty condiment to use with these puppies, fries and fish is a mixture of half ketchup and half HEINZ 57 SAUCE.

This is my Uncle Aut's hush puppy recipe. He owned and operated the CITY CAFE in LaFollette from the '40s until he retired sometime in the '70s. Mama, Dad, Joy and I would have supper there every Saturday evening. I always ordered fish, french fries and hush puppies with a NEHI orange drink. I worked there some on weekends when I was in high school, and it was hard work. Uncle Aut would arrive about 4 a.m. to get ready for the breakfast crowd, and never left before 10 p.m. after cleaning up. Of course, he fried his hush puppies on the grill, but they are just as good fixed in an iron skillet.

BLACKENED CATFISH

6 Catfish Fillets
4 Teaspoons Salt
3 Tablespoons
  Paprika
1 Teaspoon Freshly
  Ground Black
  Pepper
1 Teaspoon White
  Pepper
2 Teaspoons
Thyme
2 Teaspoons
  Oregano
1 Cup Melted
  Butter

Heat a large cast-iron skillet to very hot adding no fat or shortening. I prepare this outside on the barbecue grill because of the smoke the dish produces. Mix all the dry spices. Cut each fillet in half. Dip the fillets in butter and then sprinkle both sides with the spice blend. When the skillet is heated to almost red-hot, add the fillets, as many as the skillet will hold at a time. Cook, about three minutes to a side, depending on the thickness of the fish.

You'll think you've started a small fire, and destroyed your catfish—not so. The hot, ungreased skillet will produce a black, tasty char on the outside and the flesh underneath will be sweet and white.

Sprinkle the fish with chopped green onions and serve with coleslaw and french-fried or baked potatoes. Serves four.

117

1 Pint Fresh Oysters
¾ Single Stack NABISCO Saltines
2 Eggs, Beaten
¼ Cup Oil

When frying oysters, employ this method. Use about ¾ of a single stack of NABISCO Premium Saltines (a fancy name for crackers) crushed very fine; a food processor is handy for this. In a separate bowl, beat two eggs. Have about ¼ cup oil heated to medium in a large cast-iron skillet; you may need to add more oil as the oysters are fried. In this sequence prepare the oysters: directly from the oyster container dredge the oysters in the cracker crumbs; dip next into the egg; next, back into the crumbs; then into the skillet. Do this quickly, and they will need to be turned at almost the same time. Turn the oysters as they brown, starting with the first one you put into the oil. Serve when they have browned nicely, with french-fries, rolls, and accompanied by ketchup and seafood cocktail sauce.

Seafood wasn't readily available when I was a kid. I had never even *seen* a shrimp until we went on vacation to visit my Aunt Betty in Wilmington, North Carolina.

We brought some shrimp back once, and Mama invited my Grandfather and Grandmother Parrott to our house for supper. Mama fried the shrimp, and Paw Kelly thought they were pretty good, except he judged the tails were a little on the crunchy side, especially since he didn't have teeth.

1 Pint Oysters
  (About 3 Dozen Medium)
½ Cup Butter, Melted
½ Teaspoon Salt
Dash Of Pepper, Freshly Ground
¼ Cup Oyster Liquor
½ Cup Light Cream
3 Cups Soft Crumbs (Or Cracker
  Crumbs)
2 Tablespoons Onion, Finely
  Chopped

"He was a bold man who first ate an oyster."
Dean Swift

Grease a shallow baking dish. Drain the oysters. Crush the crumbs fine and measure into a separate one-quart bowl. Add the melted butter and mix well. Spread half the crumbs in the baking dish and place the drained oysters in a layer on top of the crumbs. Sprinkle with the finely chopped onions and season with salt and pepper. Pour ¼ of the oyster liquor and the cream over the oysters. Top with the remaining crumbs and bake for fifteen-twenty minutes at 350 degrees or until the top is lightly browned.

Oyster Stew

2 Pints Oysters
2 Pints Half & Half
1½ Tablespoons Butter
½ Tablespoon Finely
  Chopped Parsley
½ Teaspoon Onion Juice
Salt And Pepper To Taste

Strain the oysters and put the oyster liquor into a saucepan. Heat the oyster broth but do not boil. Heat the milk in the top of a double boiler over water. When both are hot, add the broth to the milk in the double boiler and stir. Add the butter and seasoning, and then add the oysters one at-a-time and continue to heat until heated through. Never allow the mixture to boil. Serve when the oysters start to swell and the edges crinkle.

Oysters are delicate creatures and by all rights should be eaten raw with horseradish sauce. However, if you insist on stewing them, because of their delicate nature, they demand to be cooked in cream or half-and-half. And please! Cook them gently, and only enough to satisfy your taste. Too much cooking, and they become tough.

THE YELLOW TOM-CAT

Like one who seizes a dog by the ears is a passer-by who meddles in a quarrel not his own. Proverbs 26:17

OF THE FIVE HALF-GROWN cats that lived around and under the front porch, the yellow tom was the one the others looked to for leadership. He was just a bit bigger than the other four, probably because he was a bit meaner and used his meanness to get more milk when he was a kitten, and now more food when the boy brought the supper scraps outside.

Several weeks ago, when they were fully kitten, and one could see only cuteness and not natural cat animosity, the boy and his sister watched and yearned to pet them as they rolled and played kitten games in the grass. But that was an impossible dream. Besides being cute, they were faster than greased lightening. Seemingly completely unaware of the children as they played or napped, if either the boy or girl moved even a quarter of an inch toward, or had even a fleeting thought about catching one of them, there was suddenly only the dust of their passage as they streaked toward the hole that gave access to underneath the porch.

From the cat viewpoint, the porch was not an edifice upon which to walk and sit, but a cool, dark sanctuary and haven for misunderstood cats. It was about fifteen feet long and maybe eight or nine feet from front to back. It was floored with painted pine planks that had shrunk just a little, as pine will, and left a tiny space between each slat. For the cats, this was perfect. They saw the natural tendency of the wood to shrink as one of God's gifts that allowed just enough sunlight to seep into their dark world so they could barely see.

The father of the children had chiseled out one concrete block at the side of the porch to allow air circulation. The cats and spiders saw this as another of God's provisions.

As the kittens grew, they lost their appeal to the boy. He was not the sort to torment God's dumb creatures, but figured they must have been put on earth for some reason other than to consume supper scraps. His dog, Penny, shared his sentiment, especially since she considered the scraps hers. Their mutual goal in life shifted from a desire to cuddle, to harassing tactics, the object of which was to discourage them from sticking their noses outside the hole when the front yard was occupied by dog or boy.

The sister, however, still saw them as objects worthy of rehabilitation. That attitude would carry over and into her adult life. Unfortunately, all this set the stage for conflict and pitted two very different cat theologies, one against the other, which resulted in an undercurrent of brother-sister friction. Even more unfortunate for the dog and boy; the sister was four years the senior, besides possessing the natural cunning of the female. The boy was not dumb, he just had not yet had the benefit of experience, and therefore was not very smart.

It was summer vacation. The day was hot, humid and still. No cars had passed on the road in front of their house for more than three hours. Occasionally they would hear a truck passing on the highway about a mile away. They sat on the porch steps playing a lackluster game of MONOPOLY. Joy (the sister) had a stack of orange $500 dollar-bills that was three times the amount that was in the bank. The boy had long ago spent his only $500 dollar-bill paying rent to the wealthy sister. He wondered silently if there might not be some connection between being keeper of the bank and being wealthy, and although not smart, he was certainly not dumb enough to express the sentiment aloud. Besides being four years older, the girl was four years bigger than he.

The cats lay sleeping in various poses in the grass around the porch, none of them more than ten feet from the protection of the hole. "Ricky, see if you can catch Tom there. Don't he look sweet?"

The boy had no desire to catch Tom, but it did gall him to see the cat and his brothers and sisters resting there in apparent contempt while he and Penny were on the porch. He knew that even in his most imaginative fantasy there was not any way to catch the yellow cat. In fact, being aware of its general disposition, he knew that if he ever *did* catch it, there would be nothing but the bottoms of his bare feet that would escape being scratched. The prospect of a sudden dive toward Tom, however, did have its appeal. For an instant, dust would boil, the dog would go berserk, the cats would scream and his mother would run to the door to see what had happened.

He dove for the cat, and everything happened just as he had envisioned it. Mama stood at the door. *"Hubert Richard Parrott!* If you don't leave those cats alone, I'm going to get my switch. Joy, I *told you* to make him leave them alone. One more thing out of you, boy, and I'm telling your Daddy when he gets home."

123

Mama left and they sat back down, watching the dust settle. "Ricky, have you ever caught Tom?"

"Nope, and I hope I never do, neither."

"What do you reckon they do under there?"

"I donno. Just set around scratching I guess. Why?"

"Well, I was just wondering, that's all. Can you see up under there?"

"Na, it's too dark," the boy answered. He was growing uncomfortable. He knew his sister well, and could tell when she had something up her sleeve.

"Wouldn't you like to know for sure what they do?"

"Yeah, I guess so. Why?"

"Why don't you look? You could stick your head right up to the hole, and probably see them."

The boy considered this. He could think of no reason not to look in the hole. What could possibly be the danger of seeing under there? Mama had said not to bother them anymore. Surely just to look would be okay.

He got on his hands and knees and put his face to the hole. Nope. Black as the ace of spades. He couldn't see a thing.

"Can't see anything," he yelled to his sister standing beside him, his voice muffled.

"Ricky, stick your head in just a little ways and maybe you can see more."

He thought about that for a while. No reason not to. It could be that there might be something interesting in there besides cats anyway. Maybe the guy that lived here before them had left some treasure in a fruit jar under there or something. There might even be a skull, like in that Hardy Boy's book he was reading.

The boy was skinny, but not skinny enough for the hole. At the suggestion, encouragement and assistance of his sister, however, he found that if he turned his head

124

sideways, it would barely clear the top and bottom of the hole and admit just the top of his shoulders. Once inside, he straightened his head and looked around.

"Gee," he thought, "its dark in here." All he could see was blackness, with just a tiny bit of light filtering through the cracks above. His mind turned from thoughts of cats and treasure to black widow spiders and snakes.

"See anything," Joy asked?

"No, It's still too dark."

"Well, wait a few minutes till your eyes get used to the dark."

For the first time in its short life, the yellow tom-cat felt fear. His sanctuary was being invaded. His heartbeat increased and his blood pressure inched upward. The boy's skinny body was obscuring the comforting square of light that until now had been their portal for re-entrance into the world of sunshine. "Maybe if I just sit here," the cat thought, "it will go away." His thoughts turned to his mother. "Maybe she'll be back in just . . . "

WHAM! WHAP! WHAM! The porch was falling in! What was left of the tom cat's meager grasp on hope was abandoned. Ten years of accumulated dirt and dust began raining down on the cats as the awful crashing continued. All thought of waiting, or hoping that Mama Cat would return, vanished in an instant. Tom's leadership evaporated. It was every cat for himself. With a corporate wild screech, five frenzied, hysterical cats rushed for the faint outline of light they could see around the boy's head.

"Aarrrrgh!" The boy screamed. What was happening? Brother Robinson had said Jesus would return in an instant—we know not when—but he had never imagined he would have his head stuck in a cat-hole when it happened. "Oh, sweet Jesus, let me be truly saved and headed for thy kingdom."

The boy and all five cats decided simultaneously they

no longer wanted to be under the porch, and met at the hole. Neither dumbness or stupidity entered into the boy's calculation as he removed himself. Speed was his only consideration; except he forgot to turn his head sideways. He ended up, his nose and the back of his head scraped, sitting on his hind-end at the hole, a human runway for five mad cats as they tore toward the protecting fence hedge, setting a cat record for speed, which has yet to be equalled.

His sister continued to beat gleefully on the porch floor with the broom Mama had told her earlier to sweep with.

Mama stood at the door, pale, and for once speechless. The dog, also knowing the sister well, and being much smarter and more experienced than the boy, had long since divined what the outcome of all this was going to be and had hid under a bush at the opposite side of the house.

Much later, after mercurochrome, chocolate chip cookies and lemonade had been judiciously used to calm the situation, the boy lay on his bed and wondered if his sister was of a type, and if all girls were basically of the same temperament. He decided they probably were and made a vow to religiously avoid them. If a fellow's own sister could treat one so, there was no telling what a stranger could be capable of.

The cats stayed away for days, debating new leadership roles. Tom never recovered and stayed well away from the house except at night.

What separates this lemonade from others is making a syrup by boiling together the sugar and water. This assures that all the sugar is dissolved.

Worldwide, lemons rank third in tonnage to all citrus fruits produced. The United States is number one in production. Three fourths of our harvest comes from California, and the balance mostly from Arizona.

Lemonade

½ Gallon Water (8 Cups)
12-16 Tablespoons Lemon Juice
32 Tablespoons Sugar
1 Teaspoon Salt

To make a little more than ½ gallon of lemonade, boil together the sugar and water for two minutes. Chill the mixture until cool and then add the freshly squeezed lemon juice and salt. Stir thoroughly, and pour into tall glasses filled with ice. Garnish with thin slices of the lemon.

CHOCOLATE CHIP COOKIES

⅔ Cup CRISCO Shortening
⅔ Cup Butter
1 Cup Granulated Sugar
1 Cup Brown Sugar, Packed
2 Eggs
2 Teaspoons Vanilla Extract
3 Cups Flour
1 Teaspoon Soda
1 Teaspoon Salt
1½-2 Cups Chopped Nuts
2 Packages Semi-Sweet
  Chocolate Morsels (6 Ounce)

Preheat oven to 375 degrees. Thoroughly mix the shortening, butter, eggs, sugar and vanilla. Blend in the remaining ingredients. Drop dough by rounded teaspoons, about two inches apart onto an ungreased baking sheet. Bake eight-ten minutes or until lightly browned.

Besides being very nice to eat, home-made chocolate chip cookies are valuable for many other things, one of those being useful to soothe hurt feelings.

I personally like my cookies on the crunchy side, instead of soft. If you like your cookies crunchy, store them in an air-tight container.

Mama thought kids benefited more from hot oatmeal or cream of wheat for breakfast than they ever could from all the knowledge of medical science. I grew up, consequently, hating oatmeal, until eighteen years ago when Pat made some of these cookies.

¾ Cup Sugar
¼ Cup Brown Sugar
½ Cup Butter, Softened
½ Teaspoon Vanilla Extract
1 Egg
¾ Cup All-Purpose Flour
½ Teaspoon Baking Soda
½ Teaspoon Cinnamon
¼ Teaspoon Salt
1½ Cups Quick-Cooking Oats
½ Cup Raisins
¾ Cup Chopped Pecans

Preheat oven to 375 degrees. In a large bowl beat sugar, ¼ cup tightly packed brown sugar and butter until well creamed. Add the vanilla and egg and blend well. Stir in flour, soda, cinnamon and salt and blend well. Stir in the rolled oats, raisins and ¾ cup pecans. Drop by rounded teaspoons, about two inches apart, onto greased cookie sheets. Bake for eight-ten minutes or until the edges start to become golden brown. Cool for two-three minutes before removing from the sheets. Makes about 40 cookies.

Mama's Skillet Fried Chicken

1 Frying Chicken
2 Eggs, Beaten
Salt
All-purpose Flour
Shortening

Wash well and cut up the chicken. Dip the pieces into the beaten egg, and season well with salt. Put about two cups of flour into a paper bag, place the chicken in the bag, four pieces at-a-time and shake vigorously. Put a good amount of shortening into a heavy iron skillet and melt. When the shortening is hot, reduce the heat a little and fry the chicken slowly. Turn frequently and cook for about 30 minutes, uncovered. After the pieces are browned, place a lid over the skillet and simmer for about fifteen minutes.

Any left-over chicken should be kept in the refrigerator, uncovered for lunch or a late-night snack. This goes well with potato salad on a picnic.

Mama says the secret ingredient for making fried chicken special is simple: use plenty of salt.

7 Medium Potatoes
4 Hard Boiled Eggs
1 Large Onion, Chopped Fine
1 Cup Mayonnaise
½ Cup Sour Cream (Optional)
½ Cup Pickle Relish
1 Teaspoon Celery Seed
1 Teaspoon Salt (To Taste)
¾ Teaspoon Black Pepper
Paprika

Serve this mayonnaise based potato salad with fried chicken, baked ham, or accompanying any entree that can be served cold. If you take it on a picnic, however, be sure to provide an ice chest to keep it properly cooled.

Wash but do not peel the potatoes. Cover with water and cook for 30-45 minutes or until tender. Let the potatoes cool completely, and then peel and dice. Blend the potatoes with all the remaining ingredients except the mayonnaise. Add mayonnaise, a tablespoon at-a-time until the potato salad reaches the desired consistency and texture. Use more than the called-for one cup if necessary. Sprinkle paprika on top of the potato salad for appearance. Refrigerate any unused portions.

131

Deviled Eggs

6 Hard Boiled Eggs
1 Small Onion, Minced
1 Tablespoon Pickle
   Relish
1 Heaping Tablespoon
   Mayonnaise To
   Moisten
½ Teaspoon Salt
¼ Teaspoon Pepper

Boil the eggs in water with a tablespoon of salt added. The salt will make it easier to peel the eggs. Bring to a boil, reduce heat and cook at medium-low for fifteen minutes. Drain, cover with cold water and allow to cool. Peel the eggs carefully, and using a sharp knife cut them in half length-wise. Remove the yolks and use a fork to mash and mix the yolks well with the other ingredients, adding salt and pepper to taste. Be careful though, for some reason it is easy to get the filling too salty; I suppose its because of the salt in the mayonnaise.

Add a little more mayonnaise if necessary. Fill the hollows of the egg white halves with this mixture and then sprinkle with paprika. Refrigerate the deviled eggs covered until serving time.

Boston Baked Beans

2 Cups Dried White
   Beans
2 Tablespoons Molasses
¼ Pound Salt Pork
½ Onion, Chopped
1 Teaspoon Salt

Soak the beans over-night, drain and cover with cold water, bring to a boil and continue boiling for about twenty minutes. Drain the beans, reserving the bean soup, and place in a pot or dish. Add pork, molasses and salt. Cover with the reserved soup and bake covered in a 300 degree oven for about six hours. Remove the cover and brown before serving. Makes about five servings.

Hot Potato Salad

6-7 Medium
  Potatoes
4 Strips Bacon
⅓ Cup Chopped
  Onion
¼ Cup Chopped
  Celery
½ Cup Pickle
  Relish Or 1
  Large Dill
  Pickle, Chopped
¼ Cup Water
½ Cup Mild
  Vinegar
¾ Teaspoon Sugar
½ Teaspoon Salt
Large Dash Paprika
¼ Teaspoon Dry
  Mustard

Use red potatoes or mature Idahos for this dish. Wash and scrub the potatoes, cover with water and cook covered in a saucepan until tender. When the potatoes are done, peel and cube them into a serving bowl. Fry the bacon, remove it from the skillet and reserve, and in the drippings, sauté the onion and celery. Crumble the bacon into the cubed potatoes. When the onion is clear, add the pickle relish or dill pickle. In a separate saucepan, heat the water, vinegar, sugar, salt, paprika and dry mustard to boiling. Carefully add this mixture to the onion-celery mixture in the skillet, stir and then gently blend this into the cubed potatoes. Serve at once with your meal, but any leftovers may be served cold.

Old Fashioned Hot Potato Salad

½ Cup Granulated Sugar
1 Teaspoon Salt
1 Teaspoon Dry Mustard
1 Tablespoon Cornstarch
2 Egg Yolks, Well Beaten
½ Cup Water
1 Tablespoon Butter
½ Cup Vinegar
½ Teaspoon Celery Seed
3 Eggs, Hard Boiled
6-8 Irish Potatoes, Cooked

Cook the potatoes, unpeeled. Allow them to cool and then remove the skins and dice. Coarsely chop the boiled eggs. To make the dressing, mix all the dry ingredients. Add the water to the beaten eggs, blend, and then mix with the dry ingredients. Cook the mixture in a saucepan until it starts to thicken. Add the butter and vinegar. Continue to cook, stirring, until the mixture reaches a pleasing texture. Place the potatoes and eggs into a serving bowl, pour the hot mixture over them and lightly blend. Serve hot.

This recipe came from a friend who will turn 91 this year. The letter she wrote with the recipe said, "I'll write what I think makes my potato salad better than some I've tried. Most folks add everything to what they call potato salad; bacon crumbled up, pickles, celery and who knows what-all. I've been eating the kind Mama made for nearly 90 years. I have had many statements, 'you make the *best* potato salad!"

Instead of leaving the potatoes cubed, she mashes them before adding the eggs and dressing.

PICKLED SUMMER SQUASH

8½ Cups Yellow Summer Squash, Sliced Thinly (About 3 Pounds)
2 Quarts Water
⅔ Cup Pickling Salt
3 Cups Granulated Sugar
2 Cups White Vinegar
1¼ Tablespoon Celery Seeds
1 Tablespoon Mustard Seeds
2½ Cups Chopped Green Sweet Peppers
2 Cups Onion, Sliced Thinly And Separated Into Rings
1 Jar (4 Ounce) Diced Pimento, Drained (Or, 1 Cup Chopped Red Sweet Pepper)

Place the sliced squash in a large container (do not use aluminum). Blend the water and salt, stirring until the salt completely dissolves and then pour it over the squash. Cover with a clean cloth, let stand one hour, and then drain. Combine the sugar, vinegar and celery seeds in another large pot. Add the squash, green pepper and all the remaining ingredients. Bring to a boil. Remove from the heat and pack the hot mixture (but not the liquid) into pint sterilized, hot jars, filling to ½-inch of the top. Finish by pouring the hot liquid from the vegetable mixture into the jars, covering the relish. Remove any air bubbles and wipe the jar rims. Cover with lids and screw on the bands. Process in a boiling-water bath for fifteen minutes. Yield: four-five pints.

POTATO CHEESE SOUP

3 Medium Potatoes, Cubed
2 Cups Boiling Water
2-3 Cups Milk
3 Tablespoons Butter
½ Large Onion, Chopped
2 Tablespoons Flour
1 Teaspoon Salt
Dash Cayenne Pepper
1 Tablespoon Parsley
1 Cup Cheddar Cheese, Grated

Cook the potatoes in boiling, salted water until tender and then strain, reserving the liquid. Measure the liquid and add enough milk to make 3½ cups. Scald this mixture and add it back to the potatoes. In a skillet, melt the butter, add the chopped onion and sauté for five minutes. Add the flour and seasonings to the onion-butter mixture and then combine with the potatoes. Cook for three minutes. Add the grated cheese and stir quickly until smooth. Add chopped parsley as a garnish and serve while very hot.

Potatoes are one of the foods that are native to the Americas and did not come from Europe with our forefathers.

Yes! Believe me. Potatoes did not come from Ireland to here, but the reverse.

Further, think about this, another native American food is the *tomato*. I wonder what they ate with their spaghetti in Italy before Columbus came in search of the trade routes they needed for spices?

GRILLED CAJUN T-BONE STEAK

T-Bone Steaks, ¾-Inch Thick   Meat Tenderizer
Garlic Cloves   ZATARAIN'S CREOLE SEASONING
       PAM Butter Flavored Cooking Spray

BLACKENING SEASONING

3 Tablespoons Paprika   3 Teaspoons Thyme
1½ Teaspoon Black Pepper   3 Teaspoons Oregano
       ¾ Teaspoon Cayenne Pepper (Optional)

Preheat your grill to its highest setting. Combine the ingredients for the blackening seasoning and put into a shaker with large holes. Follow this order: rub each steak with crushed garlic cloves; on each steak, shake about ¼ teaspoon each of the meat tenderizer and then the Creole seasoning; spray each steak with cooking spray and then shake about ½ teaspoon of the blackening seasoning over each, coating evenly. Turn the steaks and repeat all the steps in the same sequence. Grill 2½-3 minutes on each side for medium cooked steaks, turning with tongs. Top each steak with a teaspoon of equally mixed anchovy paste and softened butter and serve with a baked potato.

The high heat and distinct layers of seasonings will cause the outside of the steak to have a black, crisp, charred crust, leaving the inside pink and tender. You may also achieve the same effect by using a heavy cast-iron skillet. Follow the same directions, but use more of the cooking spray (on the meat, not the skillet). Heat the skillet, ungreased, until it is almost ashen hot, about ten minutes. Add the steaks to the heated skillet and char on each side for about three-four minutes. If you use this method, expect a lot of smoke.

CHICKEN POT PIE

1 Medium (About 3 Pound)
  Broiler/Fryer
5 Medium Potatoes, Pared
5 Stalks Celery
½ Pound Carrots, Cleaned
1 Can Peas, Drained (17 Ounce)
½ Cup Butter
⅔ Cup All-Purpose Flour
1 Cup Milk
1 Chicken Flavored Bullion Cube
10-12 Baked Biscuits

Using the *Riz Biscuit* recipe, prepare and bake 10-12 biscuits, but remove them from the oven just before they brown. This will be about ½ the recipe. The remaining dough can be frozen for later use.

Put the chicken, 1 teaspoon salt and ½ teaspoon pepper in a kettle and cover with water. Bring to a boil, cover the pot and cook at medium-low heat for 1 hour. Remove the chicken, let cool and separate from the bones, cutting into bite-sized pieces.

Dice the potatoes, celery and carrots. Place the vegetables into the chicken broth and simmer until tender. Drain and keep 3 cups of the broth. Combine the chicken pieces and cooked vegetables and pour them carefully into 13 x 9-inch baking dish. Melt the butter in a saucepan over low heat. Add flour, stirring until smooth. Cook for 1 minute, stirring constantly. Now, gradually stir in the milk, 3 cups of reserved broth, and the bullion cube. Increase the heat to medium and cook, stirring constantly, until thickened and bubbly. Add the remaining 2 teaspoons of salt and the remaining ½ teaspoon pepper. Pour the sauce over the chicken-vegetable mixture.

Bake at 400° for 45 minutes. Carefully place the biscuits on top of your chicken pie mixture and bake for an additional 8-10 minutes until the biscuits are golden.

SHEPHERD'S PIE

4 Tablespoons
  Cooking Oil
3 Tablespoons
  Chopped Onion
2 Tablespoons
  Chopped Green
  Pepper
½ Cup Diced
  Celery
1 Cup Cooked
  Hamburger,
  Ground Beef Or
  Ground Chuck
4 Tablespoons
  Flour
2 Cups Milk
½ Cup Diced
  Cooked Carrots
2-3 Cups Mashed
  Potatoes

Slowly brown onion, pepper, celery and hamburger in cooking oil, stirring constantly. Add the flour slowly, stirring constantly, until brown. Add the remaining ingredients and heat thoroughly. Pour into a shallow, well-oiled baking dish and cover with a layer of well seasoned mashed potatoes. Dot with butter and bake in a 400 degree oven until well browned. This will make about six servings.

If you use hamburger, which is higher in fat than ground beef or chuck, reduce the cooking oil by one tablespoon.

MEAT LOAF

1 Pound Ground Beef
¼ Teaspoon Celery Seed
½ Cup Chopped Onion
⅓ Cup Milk
¼ Cup Bread Crumbs
1 Egg, Beaten
1 Tablespoon Worcestershire
  Sauce
3 Tablespoon Brown Sugar
¾ Cup Catsup
½ Teaspoon Salt, Or To Taste
¼ Teaspoon Black Pepper

In a large bowl combine the ground beef, celery seed, onion, milk, bread crumbs, egg, Worcestershire sauce, salt and pepper. Shape into a loaf and place on a wire rack over a foil-lined pan. Combine the brown sugar and catsup, and pour it over the top of the meat loaf. Bake in a 350 degree oven for 45 minutes. Serves four.

Both Mama and Pat make very good meat loaf, but in my mind and imagination, the best that was ever made must have been from the hand of Aunt Bee. Remember Opie's face when she sat down the serving dish for him, Barney and Andy?
I'll bet Bee's was much like this recipe.

3½ Pounds Pork Ribs
1 Large Onion, Quartered
1 Quart Homemade Kraut or
   1 Quart Refrigerated
   Store-Bought Kraut In A Jar

Please do not use store-bought kraut that is packaged in a metal can. You can find it in a glass jar or a plastic bag in the cooler section of your grocery store. It is usually displayed with the refrigerated Kosher dill pickles.

Cut the meat into portions of 3-4 ribs each. Place them into a heavy pot or kettle and brown. You might want to spray the pot first with just a little cooking spray, or add a touch of oil. Add 2-2½ cups of water and the onion and bring to a boil. Skim off any foam. Reduce the heat, cover the pot and lightly boil until the meat has fully cooked and is tender. Add the kraut. If you must use commercial kraut in a metal can, drain it first. Continue to cook uncovered for about 30 minutes, or until the broth is relatively thick.

For a nice "German" flavor, add about ½ cup of thinly sliced apples and ¼ teaspoon of Caraway seeds. Apples and onions? Yep. That's what I thought too.

141

5-7 Fresh Parsnips
2 Tablespoons Bacon
   Drippings
½ Cup Sugar
½ Teaspoon Salt
1 Cup Water

Wash the parsnips, remove the ends, peel and slice crossways about ⅛-inch thick. Add bacon drippings to a cast-iron skillet and heat. Add the sliced parsnips, add salt and sprinkle sugar over the parsnips. Add water, cover and cook until all the liquid is gone, stirring occasionally. As the liquid cooks away, check frequently to keep from burning. When the liquid is gone, remove the lid and brown.

Be careful the parsnips don't burn, " 'cause that sugar'll let 'em burn right quick."

FRIED SWEET POTATOES

6-8 Yellow Sweet
   Potatoes
¼ Cup Hot Bacon
   Drippings
½ Teaspoon Salt
½ Cup Sugar
1 Cup Water

Peel and slice the sweet potatoes crossways and add them to hot bacon drippings. Salt to taste and sprinkle sugar over the potatoes. Add water, cover tightly and cook over medium heat until all the liquid is gone. Remove the lid and fry slowly until light brown. Stir often as the sugar will cause the potatoes to burn easily.

There is not a lot that can be said about, or done to a carrot that is interesting. This recipe, however does not lend credence to that statement. If you thought you did not like carrots, try this dish. It is very nice, but be sure to serve it immediately, for it suffers as it cools.

9 Carrots, Scraped And Each Cut Into Four Pieces, Length-Wise
¾ Cup Water
¼ Cup Granulated Sugar
1 Heaping Tablespoon Brown Sugar
1½ Tablespoons Fresh Lemon Juice With Pulp
⅛ Teaspoon Salt
2 Tablespoons Butter

Cook the carrots in water until tender and then drain. In a saucepan melt the butter and then add the remaining ingredients. Bring just to a boil and pour over the cooked carrots arranged on a serving plate. Serve while very hot.

143

DELICIOUS SOUR CREAM ROLLS

1 Package Active Dry Yeast
¾ Cup Butter
6 Sups Sifted All-Purpose Flour
½ Cup Lukewarm Water
2 Eggs
1 Cup Sour Cream
1¼ Teaspoon Salt
½ Cup Sugar

Sprinkle the dry yeast over a little lukewarm water to soften. Melt the butter and allow it to cool. Beat the eggs until they are thick, then into the eggs, stir the melted butter, sour cream and the yeast mixture. Sift the flour, salt and sugar together. Beat the flour mixture a little at-a-time into the egg mixture until it is smooth, and knead the dough thoroughly. Place the dough into a greased bowl, cover and let rise in a warm spot until double. Punch down, shape into little balls and let them rise on a greased baking sheet. When the rolls are doubled in size, bake in a preheated 375° oven for 10-15 minutes. This recipe makes about 18 rolls. The dough can also be rolled out, sprinkled with melted butter, sugar and cinnamon, rolled into cylinders, sliced, raised and baked.

The sour cream in this recipe is mostly for flavor, but is an essential ingredient for several dishes you will find here, like beef stroganoff and paprika veal.

It was only lately that sour cream was commercially available in the Appalachian region. Granny (Mama's mother) in fact, probably used soured milk or cream when she found that special flavor necessary in a recipe. Before they had an ice box in which one placed blocks of ice, the dairy products were stored and kept fresh in the cool water of a spring house.

FRIED APPLES

8-10 Apples
½ Stick Butter
  (No Margarine Please)
½ Cup Sugar

Peel, core and slice the apples. The best frying apples are Granny Smith, Red Delicious and Golden Delicious. Heat the butter to medium low in a large cast-iron skillet. Add the apples, sprinkle with sugar and fry uncovered, stirring and turning often until tender and just starting to brown. Serve with a breakfast that includes biscuits, or serve with any pork dish.

COOKED APPLES

4-5 Tart Apples, Peeled, Cored and Chopped Or Sliced
½ Cup Sugar

Simply place the apples in a heavy saucepan with about ½ cup sugar (use more or less according to your preference) and cook. Some varieties of apples will cook up into a mush-like consistency, while others will retain their shape. You may add cinnamon and nutmeg to spice them up a bit.

APPLE COBBLER

3 Cups Cooked Apples   ¾-1 Cup Sugar
4 Tablespoons Butter   ¾ Teaspoon Cinnamon
Pie Crust For Cobbler

Line an 8 x 8-inch baking dish with pie dough, and allow a considerable amount to hang over the edge. Pour in the apples and sprinkle with sugar and cinnamon to taste. Dot with butter. Fold the dough over the fruit, and if the dough does not completely cover the apples, fill in the center with smaller pieces of left-over dough. Bake at 350° or until the top is golden brown.

PAT'S PERFECT APPLE PIE

Pastry For Double-Crust 9-Inch Pie   ¼ Tsp. Salt
5-6 Cups Sliced Apples   ½ Cup Brown Sugar
2 Tbsp. All-Purpose Flour   2 Tbsp. Butter
1 Tsp. Ground Cinnamon   ¼-½ Tsp. Nutmeg
1 Cup Granulated Sugar (Use ½ Cup More If Apples Are Especially Tart)

Line a nine-inch piepan with ½ the pastry rolled out to ⅛-inch thick. Arrange the apples in the unbaked shell. Combine the flour, both types of sugar, salt, cinnamon and nutmeg and sprinkle over the apples. Dot with butter. Roll out the remaining pastry and place over apples; seal and flute edges. Slash the crust in a pleasing pattern so steam can escape. Bake at 375° for 1 hour and 15 minutes or until the crust is brown and the apples are tender.

For a nice brown top, brush with one tablespoon of melted butter and sprinkle with about a tablespoon of sugar for the last five minutes of baking time.

½ Cup All-Purpose Flour
½ Cup Sugar
½ Cup Whole Milk
2 Teaspoons Baking Powder
¼ Cup Butter
3 Cups Cooked Blackberries
 (Cook Berries With ¾ Cup
 Sugar)

A cobbler is a kissing cousin to a deep dish fruit pie. Usually served with rich cream or hard sauce, try this one with vanilla ice-cream.

In an 8-inch square baking dish, melt the quarter cup of butter. In a separate bowl, mix the flour, baking powder and sugar and then stir in the milk. This will make a thick batter. Pour the batter into the baking dish with the butter and then pour the hot cooked berries on top of the batter. Bake in a 350 degree oven for about 30 minutes or until the crust browns.

When you put this dish into the oven, you may wonder if you did something wrong, or if the recipe is somehow incorrect. Fear not. Although it looks unappetizing, the berries will settle to the bottom, the batter will end up on top, and everything will turn out just right.

147

RHUBARB-STRAWBERRY COBBLER

2 Cups Rhubarb
2 Cups Strawberries
1¾ Cups Sugar
4 Tablespoons Butter
2 Tablespoons Water

CRUST

1 Cup Plain Flour
⅓ Cup CRISCO
½ Teaspoon salt
¾ Cup Milk
1 Tablespoon Baking Powder

Prepare the crust by mixing all the ingredients except the shortening and milk. Blend the dry ingredients well and cut in the shortening with two table knives until it resembles coarse cornmeal. Add the milk and work into a light dough. Dump onto a floured surface and knead until smooth. Roll out to about ⅛ inch thick. Line an 8 x 8-inch pan with the dough, reserving enough to use as a top curst after the fruit has been added. It looks nice too, to cut the top dough into strips and make a lattice.

Cut the rhubarb crosswise into about ½-inch long chunks. Cap the berries and cut them in half. Put the rhubarb and sugar into a heavy saucepan with just a couple of tablespoons of water and bring the mixture slowly to a boil; stir constantly as it will have a tendency to stick. When the mixture begins to boil remove it from the heat, stir in the berries and pour into your cobbler crust. Cover with a top crust and bake at about 350 degrees until nice and brown, about 45 minutes.

Mama's Rice Pudding

This recipe, true to Mama's character will use up any cooked rice left-over from breakfast. Her philosophy; "use it up—wear it out."

¾ Cup Cooked Rice
1 Cup Sugar
3 Eggs, Yolks And Whites
    Separated
1 Large Can Evaporated Milk (12
    Ounce)
½ Teaspoon Cinnamon
½ Teaspoon Nutmeg
⅔ Cup Raisins
1½ Teaspoon Vanilla Extract

Combine the rice, sugar, egg yolks, evaporated milk, cinnamon, nutmeg and raisins. Cook in the top of a double boiler over boiling water until thick. Remove from the heat and add vanilla. Beat the egg whites until stiff and fold into the pudding mixture. Sprinkle the top with a tablespoon of sugar mixed with a bit of nutmeg. Brown under the oven broiler. Serve hot.

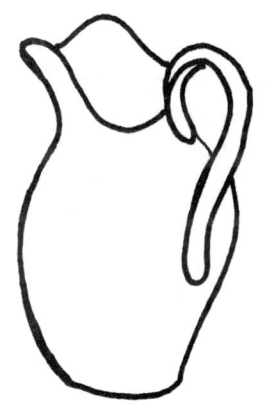

149

PAT'S RICE PUDDING

½ Cup Uncooked Rice, Washed
3 Cups Boiling Water
1½ Teaspoon Salt
1 Can BORDEN'S CONDENSED MILK
½ Cup Raisins
1 Egg, Slightly Beaten
1 Teaspoon Vanilla Extract
¼ Teaspoon Nutmeg

Place the uncooked rice, water and salt into the top of a double boiler and cook covered over rapidly boiling water for about 40 minutes. Stir in a can of BORDEN'S CONDENSED MILK and raisins. Reduce the heat and add the beaten egg slowly while stirring rapidly. Continue to cook for about six minutes while stirring constantly until the pudding will coat a spoon. Remove from the heat and stir in the vanilla extract and nutmeg. Serve warm or cold.

There is a running debate in our family concerning rice pudding. Pat thinks that it must be made with sweetened condensed milk. Beth and the dog agree. Mama starts out with cooked, left-over rice, and folds in the beaten egg whites. I like the less sweet, old fashioned kind.

I have included all three variations here. Try them out and let me know.

This is my personal favorite, not very sweet, but with more nutmeg.

1 Cup Rice (Not Instant)
5 Cups Milk (4½ Cups Plus ½ Cup)
½ Teaspoon Salt
2 Eggs, Beaten
1 Teaspoon Vanilla
⅔ Cup Raisins
½ Cup Sugar Plus 1½ Tablespoons
1 Teaspoon Cinnamon, Divided
2 Teaspoon Nutmeg, Divided

Combine the uncooked rice, 4½ cups milk, beaten eggs, salt, vanilla, sugar and raisins. Bring to a boil, reduce the heat to low and cook **covered** at medium heat for 30 minutes, stirring every ten minutes. Remove from the stove, add the remaining ½ cup milk and a half portion each of the cinnamon and nutmeg. Stir to blend and let the pudding cool for 45 minutes. After it cools, pour it into a one quart casserole dish, sprinkle with the remaining cinnamon and nutmeg blended with 1½ table spoons sugar, and brown under the oven broiler.

COTTAGE PUDDING

1¾ Cups Sifted All-Purpose Flour   1¼ Cups Sugar
2½ Teaspoons Baking Powder   1 Teaspoon Salt
⅓ Cup Soft Butter   1 Teaspoon Vanilla
1 Egg   1 Cup Heated Marmalade
1 Cup Whole Milk (Divided Into ⅔ Cup and ⅓ Cup)

You will need an 8 x 8-inch baking dish. Preheat oven to 400°. All the ingredients must be at room temperature. Into an electric mixing bowl, sift the flour, sugar, baking powder and salt. Now, add the butter and ⅔ cup milk and mix for two minutes at medium speed. Add the egg, remaining ⅓ cup milk and vanilla and mix for two minutes more, scraping the bowl constantly. Pour the batter into a greased baking dish in which you have spread heated marmalade and bake for about 25 minutes.

Cut into squares and serve with crushed or stewed fruit or your favorite Sweet Sauce.

SWEET POTATO PUDDING

3 Cups Grated Raw Sweet Potato   1 Cup Sugar
2 Eggs, Well Beaten   1 Teaspoon Salt
1 Tablespoon Butter   2 Teaspoons Cinnamon
Whole Milk Or Half & Half

Mix all the ingredients except the milk. Add enough milk, stirring, to make a thin blend. Pour into a baking dish and bake in a 350 degree oven for about 1½ hours. Yield: eight servings.

MOLASSES PUDDING

1 Egg
2 Tablespoons Sugar
½ Cup Molasses
2 Tablespoons Butter, Melted
1½ Cups Flour
½ Cup Water, Boiling
⅛ Teaspoon Salt
1 Teaspoon Baking Soda

Dissolve the baking soda in about a tablespoon of warm water. Beat the egg and sugar together until smooth. Add the butter, water, soda and molasses; mix, and then beat in the flour and salt. Place the mixture into a double boiler and let the pudding steam for one hour. Serve with Frothy Sauce.

FROTHY SAUCE

1 Cup Butter
2 Cups Powdered Sugar
⅓ Cup Sherry Cooking Wine
2 Egg Whites
¼ Cup Boiling Water

Beat the butter until it is soft, and gradually add the sugar. Continue mixing and add the **unbeaten** egg whites and then follow with the wine. When the mixture is smooth and a light color, add the boiling water, beating all the while. Place the bowl in a basin of hot water and whip briskly with a wire whisk until you have a frothy sauce.

153

MOLASSES PIE

3 Eggs, Separated
¾ Cup Brown Sugar
½ Teaspoon Nutmeg
½ Teaspoon Cinnamon
½ Teaspoon Salt
2 Tablespoons Melted Butter
1 Tablespoon Flour
1 Tablespoon Cornstarch
1½ Cup Molasses
Unbaked Pie Shell

Beat the egg yolks until thick, then add the molasses and butter. Combine the sugar, spices, salt, flour and cornstarch in a separate bowl and add them to the first mixture and mix thoroughly. Beat the egg whites until they are stiff and fold them into batter. Pour this into a pie shell and bake in a 425 degree oven for about fifteen minutes. Cover the pie with a layer of pecans, sprinkle with sugar and continue baking for fifteen minutes more.

When I was a youngster we would go way out into the country to buy molasses. Mama would pick us up early from school and it seemed we would drive for miles and miles over the crooked ridge-roads of Campbell County. We would finally end up at a sorghum press that was operated by a bored mule traveling endless circles while hitched to a pole that turned the rollers of the press. Men would feed sugar cane into it, cook the juice, strain and bottle it, and sell it for about 50¢ a quart.

154

1 Cup Suet, Finely Chopped
1 Cup Molasses
1 Cup Milk
3 Cups Flour
1 Teaspoon Soda
½ Cup Chopped Nuts
½ Cup Raisins
½ Teaspoon Salt
½ Teaspoon Ginger
½ Teaspoon Cloves
½ Teaspoon Nutmeg
1 Teaspoon Cinnamon

Sift together and mix all the dry ingredients. In a separate bowl, add the molasses and milk to the very finely chopped suet. The use of a food processor will greatly simplify the mincing of the suet. Combine the two mixtures, shape or put into a mold, and steam for three hours. Serve, topped with hard sauce.

Steamed pudding has been a favorite New England college dish since the early 1830's. It was steamed in long cylinder molds, and is called the Deacon's Hat in honor of the headgear of the trustees of some of the early Women's Seminaries. Serve as an authentic accompaniment to Corned Beef and Cabbage, page 181.

See the recipe for Johnny Bull Pudding, page 58 for more specific directions on steamed puddings.

¾ Cup Sugar   1 Can Coconut (3½ Ounce)
Dash Salt   1½ Teaspoon Vanilla
3 Tablespoons Flour   3 Egg Yolks (Separated)
   ½ Cup Water (Maybe Just A Little Less)
            Large Can Evaporated Milk
                 2 Cups Meringue
                 1 Baked Pie Shell

Combine sugar, flour and salt in the top of a double boiler. Add enough undiluted evaporated milk to make a stiff paste. Add the egg yokes and beat until smooth. Add the remaining evaporated milk and water and stir. Cook until the mixture reaches a pudding consistency, about 10-15 minutes, in a double boiler until thick, stirring so it doesn't burn. Remove from the heat and add ⅔ of the canned coconut and 1½ teaspoon of vanilla. Pour this filling into a baked pie shell, top with meringue, sprinkle with the remaining coconut and bake in a 350° oven until done, about 12-15 minutes.

I asked Mama how thick the filling should be before pouring it into the shell. She said, "Oh, about like pie filling." I would venture that the pie filling should be almost, but not quiet as thick as pudding before removing it from the stove. I never liked coconut pies that sort of spread out on the plate when sliced and served.

Pat and I go to the Cosby entrance of the Great Smokey Mountains, and hike (puff) on some of the many trails there. After several hours of walking, we like to stop at the CUB RESTAURANT, just about a mile North of the Park entrance. A fine meal is trout from their own pond followed by Coconut Cream Pie.

PIE CRUST

1½ Cups Shortening	1 Egg, Beaten
(CRISCO Butter Flavored)	1 Teaspoon Salt
3 Cups Flour, All-Purpose	1 Tablespoon Vinegar
5-6 Tablespoons Ice Water	

Combine the flour, shortening and salt in a mixing bowl. Using a pastry blender, cut the mixture until it resembles coarse crumbs. Add the beaten egg and vinegar. Continue to blend, adding ice water one teaspoon at-a-time. When the correct consistency is reached, turn onto flour-covered surface. Work the dough with your hands, *just enough* to enable you to roll it into a thin shell; this requires a delicate touch. Overworking will cause the baked crust to have a tough texture. For a custard pie, line the bottom of a piepan, crimp the edges and bake at 425° until golden brown. This makes four pie shells (bottoms only) or two top-bottom crusts, and freezes exceptionally well.

MERINGUE

3 Tablespoons Sugar	½ Cup Water
1 Tablespoon Cornstarch	3 Egg Whites
2 Drops Vanilla Extract	

Combine three tablespoons sugar, one tablespoon corn starch and ½ cup water. Cook this mixture over low heat until thick, stirring to prevent lumps. When finished, cool five minutes. Beat the egg whites until stiff and fold them into the cornstarch mixture. Add the vanilla and blend slightly. Spread the meringue over hot pie filling, sealing the edges. Bake at 350° until brown, about twelve-fifteen minutes.

Blackberry Jam Pie

3 Eggs
½ Cup Sugar
1 Cup Sour Cream
1 Tablespoon Melted
  Butter
1 Cup Blackberry Jam
1 Tablespoon Cornstarch
Pinch Salt
Unbaked Pie Shell
Meringue

Beat the egg yolks until thick, reserving the whites for meringue. Add cream, butter, and jam to the yolk mixture. Combine ½ cup sugar, salt, and cornstarch, and then add back to the first mixture. Blend thoroughly and pour into a pie shell. Bake in a 425 degree oven for about 25 minutes. Cover the pie with meringue, reduce the oven temperature to 325 degrees and bake for another twenty minutes or until slightly brown.

Raisin Pie

2 Eggs
1 Cup Sugar
2 Tablespoons Softened
  Butter
½ Cup Milk
1½ Cups Raisins
¾ Cup Chopped nuts
Unbaked 9-Inch Pie Shell

Beat the eggs until they are fluffy. Continuing to beat, gradually add the sugar, and when well blended beat in two tablespoons of softened butter. Add milk, nuts, and raisins and blend well. Pour into an unbaked pie shell and bake at 350 degrees for 35 minutes or until done.

VINEGAR PIE

Arthur Vick, retired owner and manager of the restaurant that sits at the very pinnacle of Clinch Mountain, between Bean Station and Tazwell, featured country ham and vinegar pie at his excellent establishment.

The words vinegar and pie seem to be contradictions, but this makes a surprisingly nice lemonlike desert that is good with black coffee.

2 Cups Boiling Water
¼ Cup Vinegar
1 Cup Sugar
3 Tablespoons Flour
3 Eggs
1 Teaspoon Lemon Flavoring
⅓ Teaspoon Salt
3 Tablespoons Sugar
Baked Pie Shell
Meringue

Beat the egg yolks until thick. Add one cup sugar, flour, and salt and mix thoroughly. Add the boiling water slowly, stirring constantly. Add the vinegar and cook in a double boiler until thick and smooth. Add salt and the lemon flavoring, mix and pour the filling into a baked pastry shell. Cover with meringue and bake in a 325 oven for about twenty minutes.

159

PEANUT BUTTER PIE

2½ Cups Milk, Heated
1 Cup Brown Sugar
⅓ Cup Cornstarch (Or Less)
2 Beaten Eggs
Pinch Of Salt
1 Teaspoon Butter
1 Cup Smooth Peanut Butter
1¼ Teaspoon Vanilla
Baked Pie Shell
Whipped Cream (Or Cool Whip)

Bring the milk to a boil in a saucepan. In a bowl, mix the sugar, cornstarch, eggs, salt and butter. Have the milk heated, and slowly pour it into the sugar mixture. Pour the resulting mixture back into the saucepan, bring it to a boil and boil for a few seconds. Add the peanut butter and vanilla extract. Blend until smooth. Pour this filling into a baked pie shell and chill. Top with whipped cream when ready to serve.

The peanut, of course is not really a nut, but a legume, for to be classified a nut (oops, there's a pun here somewhere) it would have to grow above ground.

Native to South America, it migrated to Europe, then to Africa. It ended up in the American colonies when placed on slave ships as food for the long voyage.

Long thought of as only fit for livestock feed, famous black scientist, Dr. George Washington Carver came up with 300 uses for this underrated pea.

Peanut butter was introduced at the 1904 World's Fair in St. Louis.

Use your choice of icing, but this does well with a sour cream frosting. This cake has a nice texture, is tasty, and very easy to make. You will probably need your largest bowl for all the mixing and combining.

2 Cups Flour
4½ Teaspoons Baking Powder
1 Teaspoon Salt
1½ Cups Sugar
1 Tablespoon Grated Orange
 Rind
¾ Cup Shortening
¾ Cup Milk
½ Cup Milk
3 Eggs
1 Teaspoon Vanilla

Sift together the first four ingredients. Add the next three ingredients and beat for two minutes with an electric mixer set at medium, until batter is well-blended and glossy. Add the last three ingredients; ½ cup milk, eggs and vanilla and beat for two minutes more with the electric mixer. Pour into a 15 x 8 x 2-inch sheet pan and bake at 350 degrees for 50-55 minutes. Cool and frost.

5 Eggs, Separated
1¼ Cups Sugar
1¼ Cups Plain Flour
Juice Of ½ Orange
1 Teaspoon Baking Powder

Beat the egg yolks, add the sugar and beat until smooth. Add the orange juice and mix well. Sift together the flour and baking powder, add it to the egg yolk mixture and stir well. Beat the egg whites until they become stiff and fold them into the batter. Bake in two layers in a 350 degree oven for 40 minutes. Cool and ice with Orange Icing.

Orange Icing

2 Egg Whites, Unbeaten
1½ Cups Sugar
5 Tablespoons Cold Water
1½ Teaspoons Corn Syrup
Juice Of ½ Orange
Rind Of ½ Orange, Grated

Add the egg whites, sugar, water and corn syrup to the upper part of a double boiler and beat with a rotary egg beater until well mixed. Place this over rapidly boiling water and continuing to beat constantly with your egg beater; cook for seven minutes or until the frosting will stand in peaks. Remove from the heat, add the juice and rind and beat until thick enough to spread.

This is Elsie's (Pat's Mama) favorite cake.

Don't use English Walnuts, they may give this cake a bitter taste. Black Walnuts, however have a distinct, unique flavor that defies written description.

Here is my walnut source. Go North from Knoxville on I-75 for 30 miles and exit at Caryville. Turn right off the ramp. If it is lunch-time, stop at the Cove Lake State Park restaurant. Continue on the 4-lane another 6 miles past the K-Mart on the left. Turn right on Dossett Lane and continue about ¼ mile to where the road ends. Park and leave your car and climb across the barrier. Go down the embankment, cross the railroad, and climb up the opposite side. The road forks here, one going to the right parameter of the cemetery, and the other to the left. Walk downhill on the right fork. There are 3 huge walnut trees across the fence and about halfway down the hill. Be careful of the empty well nearby, and watch for snakes.

APPLE-WALNUT CAKE

3 Cups All-Purpose Flour
1 Teaspoon Baking Soda
1 Teaspoon Salt
4 Eggs
1½ Cups Salad Oil
2 Cups Sugar
2 Teaspoon Vanilla Extract
4 Cups Peeled, Diced Apples
2 Cups Black Walnuts

Grease and flour a ten-inch tube pan. Preheat oven to 350°. In a medium bowl, combine flour, soda and salt; set aside. In a large mixing bowl, beat the eggs, add oil, sugar and vanilla, and beat until blended. Add the dry ingredients, then beat at medium speed for 1 minute. Fold in the apples and walnuts. Pour the batter into the tube pan, and bake for 70 minutes. Cool the cake in the pan for fifteen minutes, then remove.

163

3 Eggs
2 Cups Milk
¼ Cup Sugar
3½-4 Cups All-Purpose Flour
½ Teaspoon Salt
2 Teaspoons Baking Powder
Vegetable Oil

Beat the eggs and add sugar and milk. Sift half the flour, salt and baking powder together. Add the milk, egg and sugar mixture to the flour, beating until the resulting batter is smooth and thin enough to pour through a funnel.

Heat the oil to about 375 degrees in an eight or nine-inch iron skillet. The oil should be about ¾-inch deep. Pour about ¼ cup of the batter into the funnel, keeping your finger over the bottom hole until you are ready to drizzle the batter into the hot oil in a lace-like pattern. Let the cake brown on one side, then flip and brown the other side. This should take only about a minute and a half per side. Lift the cake from the oil, and sprinkle with powdered sugar, syrup, molasses, jelly, or jam, etc. Eat immediately. Yield: about seven-eight cakes.

I saw this written on the side of a funnel cake wagon at a state fair in Fulton County Georgia.

"**I loves my wife, I loves my baby, I loves dem funnel cakes covered with jelly.**"

Banana Bread

½ Cup Butter or
  Margarine
1 Cup Sugar
2 Eggs
1 Teaspoon Soda
4 Tablespoons Buttermilk
2 Cups Flour
3 Ripe Bananas
½ Teaspoon each;
  Cinnamon, Nutmeg,
  Ground Cloves
1 Teaspoon Vanilla
  Flavoring
½-¾ Cup Nuts
½ Cup Raisins

Combine all the ingredients except for the nuts and raisins in a large mixing bowl. Beat until well blended and then fold in the nuts and raisins. Bake in a preheated 350 degree oven in two small, or one large bread loaf pan for about 45 minutes to one hour. The loaf will split at the top. A good way to judge if the bread is done is to bake it until this split is completely finished. Check with a clean straw.

Easy Walnut Orange Rolls

2 Tablespoons Butter
½ Cup Chopped English
  Walnuts
½ Cup Orange
  Marmalade
8 Brown & Serve Rolls

Melt the butter in an 8-inch round cake pan. Sprinkle chopped English walnuts over the butter. Spread marmalade evenly over the walnuts. Place one roll, top-side down in the center of the pan. Break apart the remaining rolls and arrange the sections upside-down around the center roll. Bake at 350 degrees for about 25 minutes. Cool in the pan for a few minutes, invert, then serve on a warm plate.

1¼ Cups Sifted Flour
1 Teaspoon Salt
3 Eggs
½ Cup Sugar
1¼ Cups Chopped Candied
    Fruit
1½ Cups Chopped Nuts (Use 2
    Cups If You Like)
1 Cup Chocolate Morsels
1¼ Teaspoon Vanilla Extract
1 Teaspoon Orange Extract

Add salt to the flour and sift into a mixing bowl. In a separate bowl beat the eggs and add the sugar a little at-a-time as you continue to beat. Continue whipping until very thick. Combine the flour and salt from the first step with the candied fruit, nuts, and chocolate morsels. Into this, fold the beaten egg-sugar mixture. Add the vanilla and orange extract. Pour the batter into a lightly greased and floured loaf pan and bake in a 350 degree oven for a little over 45 minutes or until done. Serve hot out of the oven spread with butter.

Many early Appalachian communities were small and isolated and did not have the service of a regular man of God as a pastor. This need was met by a traveling evangelist, usually riding a horse or mule.

This recipe evolved from the need to whip up a quick tasty desert for God's hungry traveling shepherd who boarded with members of the local flock.

POUND CAKE

3 Sticks Butter
  (Do Not
  Substitute
  Margarine)
1 Pound Powdered
  Sugar
6 Eggs
3½ Cups Plain
  Flour
1 Teaspoon Vanilla
  Extract

Using an electric mixer, cream the butter and add powdered sugar until everything is well blended. Add the eggs, one at-a-time, beating well after each egg. Now, add your flour all at one time and beat until the batter is light and fluffy. Spoon the batter into a well buttered and floured tube pan. Bake at 350 degrees until a straw tests done, about 1¼ hours. Be careful not to over-bake, or the cake will be crumbly and dry.

LEMON POUND CAKE

3 Cups Flour
2 Cups Sugar
1 Cup Crisco
4 Eggs
1 Cup Buttermilk
½ Teaspoon Soda
½ Teaspoon Baking Powder
1 Teaspoon Vanilla
1 Teaspoon Lemon Flavor

TOPPING

¾ Cups Sugar
Juice of 2 Lemons

Cream the shortening and sugar until smooth. Add the eggs and mix well. Sift together the flour, soda and baking powder. Alternately add the flour mixture and buttermilk while mixing. Continue mixing and add vanilla flavoring and lemon flavoring to the resulting batter.

Grease and dust flour into a tube pan. Turn the pan upside down and whack it once on the bottom. Pour the batter into the pan and bake at 350 degrees for 1 hour. About 30 minutes before cake is done, dissolve the sugar in the lemon juice. When you remove the cake from the oven, pour the lemon-sugar topping over the cake while it is still hot.

I found this recipe written on the back of a 1950's PEOPLES NATIONAL BANK, LaFollette, Tennessee counter check. Mama says it was given to her by Mrs. Conner, my high school Civics teacher.

BETH'S POUND CAKE

2 Cups Butter	2 Tbsp. Fresh Lemon Juice
(No Margarine)	2 Tsp. Cream Of Tarter
3 Cups All-Purpose Flour	1¼ Tbsp. Vanilla
½ Teaspoon Soda	10 Eggs, Separated
3 Cups Granulated Sugar	¼ Teaspoon Salt

Grease a tube pan with butter, sprinkle flour inside, turn it upside down and whack it on the bottom once. Combine the flour, soda and half the sugar and sift the mixture into a large bowl. Add the soft butter to the dry ingredients and blend. Add the lemon juice and ten egg *yolks*. Add them one at-a-time and blend after each.

In a separate bowl, beat the egg *whites* with ¼ teaspoon salt until peaks are formed. Next, add the rest of the sugar a bit at-a-time as you continue beating. Fold in the cream of tarter. Pour the egg white mixture over the flour-sugar mixture and with a wide spatula, fold it in very gently. Pour this batter into the tube pan. Whack the bottom of the pan on the counter top a few times to remove air bubbles (don't turn it upside down this time).

Bake the cake in a preheated 300° oven for an hour and 15 minutes. Do not open the door to check the progress of the cake. After the cake has baked for the recommended time, remove it and stick a clean straw all the way to the bottom. If no crumbs cling to the straw, turn the oven off and put the cake back in for another 15 minutes. If, however, the straw had crumbs clinging to it, bake the cake another 15 minutes in the 300° oven, and *then* turn the oven off and let it stand for 15 minutes inside the cooling oven. When you put the cake into the oven that has been turned off, it will shrink slightly from the sides of the pan.

Remove the cake from the oven and allow to stand in the tube pan for ten minutes before turning it out on a plate.

SWEET POTATO BREAD

1 Large Sweet Potato
1 Stick Butter (Not Margarine)
5 Eggs, Beaten
½ Cup Brown Sugar
½ Teaspoon Baking Soda
1 Teaspoon Salt
1 Teaspoon Cinnamon
1 Cup Half & Half
2 Cups Cornmeal
½ Cup Chopped Pecans
½ Cup Raisins (Optional)

The sweet potato in the United States, except in the South, is usually regarded not as a staple vegetable, but as a holiday side dish. World wide, however, it is the third leading vegetable crop.

It is, incidentally, a member of the morning-glory family.

Bake the sweet potato, peel and mash up enough to make two cups. Mix together the potato and butter. In a separate bowl beat the eggs with the sugar, baking soda, cinnamon and salt. Now, add this to the potato and butter mixture. Beat in the half-and-half, cornmeal, nuts and raisins. Pour this into a buttered 9 x 9-inch baking pan and bake at 350 degrees for 50-60 minutes. Cut into squares and serve warm with butter.

GROWING

Night and day, whether he sleeps or gets up, the seed sprouts and grows, though he does not know how. Mark 4:27

THE SEASON IS JUST ON THE edge of some tangible reality, but undecided about what to do. Late summer is tottering on the verge of being or not being, hesitant of the bittersweet change from growing, to slow mellowing; wondering if it should, after all, go from pliant green to brittle, rust fall.

The first chill has crept into the mornings and late evenings. Folks are digging deep into their closets, looking for warm jackets and sweaters slightly touched with the sharp spice of mothballs and cedar. For some reason they choose those of red and brown shades or with plaid flannel linings, for those seem somehow softer and warmer.

The trees skirting the edges of the dying corn fields and mountains are still green at first glance, but if the day is clear, and you look toward the leaf-rounded profile of the mountains and slightly unfocus your gaze, seeing the whole instead of the specific, you may sense the light rust-orange haze of approaching fall. It lays like a haze,

171

especially in the deeper hollows, and beckons the boy to come feel the promised chill.

It is early September, 1964. As the season hangs at the edge of some new reality, the boy too, totters on the verge of change, unaware of, but never-the-less seeking to confirm and solidify one reality before he moves into another.

He is standing at the crest of the highest foothill before the start of the forest of the mountains, and perceives all this in one deep intake of breath, finding the knowledge hidden in the smell and taste of the predawn air.

The small 20-gauge, single shot shotgun rests in the crook of his arm, the barrel pointed to the ground as Pap taught him, as he moves cautiously from under the tree. He has been waiting there for almost an hour, anticipating the first faint light of the false dawn to give substance to the trees that mark the beginning of the Cumberland Mountain timber. You must be inside the woods before the sun rises, because squirrels sleep too, and rise with the sun. If you lay in bed and wait till morning to go to the woods, the squirrels, now awake, will hear and see you long before you enter the trees. Hearing, they hide and wait for the intruder to leave. Few early risers bring home meat.

Moving across the last 100 yards of meadow, he enters the canopy of the trees. It is still almost dark, but he has been here before, and knows well the path leading to the huge scaly-barked hickory tree about 300 yards further into the woods. The trail follows a hollow, but leads steadily uphill. He is thankful for the old army field jacket with the wool lining. This is probably the coldest day they have had so far this year, and if it were fully daylight, he knows he could see his warm breath condense in the chill morning air.

The boy moves slowly, careful not to step on and

break sticks, and places his feet deliberately straight down on the leaves instead of moving through them. Though not yet stirring, the squirrels he hunts will stay in their nests if they hear movement before light.

He walks almost to the hickory tree, sits, and leans against the base of another as the sun continues its rise behind and over his right shoulder. It filters through the leaves, giving everything a golden-emerald cast. Silent before, the mountain begins to come to life. Somewhere over in the next hollow he hears something moving heavily through the brush and leaves, probably a dog or deer. The tree leaves give a quiet swish as the squirrels begin moving around. Sometimes there is a moderately loud rustle as one jumps from one tree branch to another.

Still he sits, waiting, listening to the increasing activity around him. Now! He hears something that sounds like rain, but knows it isn't rain, but small pieces of hickory nuts hitting the leaves below the big tree. They have started cutting now, sitting in the giant hickory, gnawing on the hard covering of the nuts, the pieces falling to the ground. He knows he can now move with more freedom, for the squirrels are too engrossed in feeding to pay as much attention to movement as they did earlier.

He quietly slips two shells from his pocket and starts to move toward the tree. It is fully daylight now, and the woods are alive with the sound of game staring to feed. There must be eight or ten squirrels in the big hickory. One moves and that causes another to change position. Watching those, he sees the slight movement of another higher up and to his right. Raising the gun, he looks across the barrel at the squirrel nearest the trunk, squeezes the trigger and feels it jump in his hands as it fires. Reflex causes him to hit the break lever. The spent shell is ejected and he feeds another into the chamber, raises the old gun and fires at the second squirrel as it runs out the branch toward the next tree. Again he ejects and reloads and swings toward the third squirrel that was higher and to the right of the first two. He spots it headed down the trunk, leads it slightly and fires again.

With the first shot, the tree had exploded with jumping, fleeing squirrels. Only about eight seconds had passed since the first one fell, but now the whole forest is absolutely silent. He knows the hunting is over for the morning. It will take hours for them to start moving again. He had only three shells anyway, and three squirrels were all they needed for supper.

The boy moves to the base of the tree and picks up the game, putting it into a towsack and tying it to his belt. They are young and fat. Pap will clean them and cooked with dumplings they will make a fine meal. He moves back down the mountain, moving toward home and some of Mama's good coffee and bacon.

Walking, the weight of the three squirrels bumping his leg, he starts thinking about tomorrow. This will probably be his last trip to the mountain this year. Mama, Dad and he will be driving to Knoxville to a place the form-letter called East Stadium Hall. He wonders what it will be like, sharing a room with someone he has never met, attending classes surrounded by kids he has never known. He anticipates the freedom with eagerness, but dreads being away from the familiar.

Christmas will be here pretty soon, he thinks, and Joy will be home from finishing Nurse's Training. Mama will make the divinity and fudge, the pecan cake, and that deliciously savory dressing.

Arriving at the crest of a hill, he stops to rest and looks toward the highway. Another two miles. Sure doesn't seem as far coming as going back.

The boy unbuttons the tattered jacket, shifts the gun to his other shoulder, moves down the hill, and quietly starts singing Roy Orbison's *Oh, Pretty Woman*.

Squirrel And Dumplings

2 Young Squirrels,
  Cleaned And
  Cut Into Serving
  Pieces
3-Inch Piece Salt
  Pork
½ Teaspoon Salt
¼ Teaspoon
  Pepper

Dumplings

1½ Cups Plain
  Flour
2 Teaspoons
  Baking Powder
¼ Teaspoon Salt
3 Tablespoons
  Shortening
¼ Cup Milk

Cut the shortening into all the dry ingredients with two table knives and add enough milk to make a soft dough. Turn out onto a floured surface, and knead just a few times until the dough is no longer sticky. Roll out to about ¼ inch thick and cut into strips about 1½ inches wide.

Cover the meat with water in a large saucepan, bring to a boil, reduce the heat to medium and cook covered until the squirrel is tender. When done remove the meat from the broth, bring liquid to a full boil and add the dumplings three or four at a time. Shake the pan, if needed, but do not stir. Cover and cook each batch of dumplings for about five minutes. Place the dumplings with their broth over the meat on a platter to serve.

If you prefer your squirrel with gravy instead of dumplings, follow the same recipe except when the meat is done, remove it from the broth and thicken it with about two tablespoons of flour that has been mixed with ½ cup milk. Add it to the broth and cook over medium heat until thick. Pour over the squirrel and serve.

175

FRIED SQUIRREL

2 Young Squirrels, Dressed
   And Cut Into Serving Pieces
½ Cup Flour, Plus 2 Tablespoons
   Separate
½ Teaspoon Salt
¼ Teaspoon Ground Pepper
¼ Cup Crisco Shortening
3 Cups Milk

Put the flour, salt and pepper into a paper bag. Add about half the meat at-a-time to the bag and shake vigorously to coat. In a large iron skillet heat to medium-high about ¼ cup Crisco and fry, turning to brown on all sides. When the meat is done, remove to a platter and remove all the pan drippings except for three tablespoons. Reduce the heat to medium and to the drippings add two tablespoons flour and the seasoning mixture that is left in the paper bag. Stir until browned and add three cups of milk and continue cooking, stirring constantly until the gravy is thick. Serve the gravy in a separate bowl.

I asked Mama if she had fixed any squirrel lately. She said, "no, these are town squirrels around here and they wouldn't be any account. You've got to have a mountain squirrel if it's going to be any good."

176

BACKBONES AND RIBS WITH POTATOES

At hog butchering time, the tenderloin, liver, backbones and ribs and other choice cuts were kept and used fresh and the balance was cured. This dish is best using fresh pork. You may not be able to find meat at the local grocery labeled backbones and ribs, but a package labeled "country style ribs" will do nicely.

3 Pounds Meaty Pork Ribs, Backbones
1 Whole Large Onion, Peeled
Potatoes

Place the meat, cut into pieces into a heavy pot and brown slightly. Add about two cups of water and the onion. Bring to a full boil, and skim off any foam. Reduce the heat, cover, and boil lightly until the meat is fully cooked. Throw away the onion or give it to the dog. Add the potatoes, quartered, and continue to cook for about 30 minutes or until the potatoes are cooked through and the flavors have blended. The broth should be cooked down to a small amount, and just start to thicken.

Chicken And
Rolled Dumplings

3-4 Pound Chicken
½ Teaspoon Salt
Pepper To Taste
2 Cups Plain Flour
⅓ Cup Shortening
Milk Or Water

Cook the chicken in water for about one hour, or until tender. Add the salt and pepper to the chicken, and not the dumplings. When finished, remove the chicken from the broth and allow to cool.

Cut the shortening into the flour, add milk (do not use buttermilk) and mix. Roll out on a floured surface to about ¼ inch thick and cut into strips. Reheat the chicken broth to boiling and drop in the dumplings one at-a-time. Cook for about 15-20 minutes. Meanwhile, remove the chicken from the bones and add to the dumplings when they are almost done.

Jody Brown's says his great grandmother, Mama Jewel DeFriese was a great dumpling cook. Instead of using milk or water to make up the dough for the dumplings, she would use some of the chicken broth. And, she said you want your dumplings to have some character instead of having the texture of biscuits. "Honey, if I want to make a biscuit, I'll make a biscuit; but these are dumplin's."

178

About Two Pones Cornbread
4-5 Leftover Biscuits
8-10 Crumbled Leftover Rolls
4 Hard Boiled Eggs, Chopped
Giblets Of Turkey, Cooked And
  Chopped
1 Large Onion, Chopped
1½ Tablespoons Sage, Crumbled
  Fine
1 Cup Celery, Chopped
1 Quart Turkey Or Chicken
  Broth, Boiling

In a large bowl, crumble cornbread, biscuits and rolls. You *must* use the cornbread, and it can be saved from several days ahead, but for the biscuits and rolls, any other bread you have is okay. Mix all the ingredients very well. Bring the broth to a boil and add to the mixture a little at-a-time, blending very well. Add the broth until the dressing is uniformly moist but not soggy. Serve hot. This reheats well.

Until we married, poor Pat had never eaten dressing that was not baked. Don't let that fact influence your decision to try this wonderful dressing. If you can find someone who grows and dries their own sage, use it. The spice measurements are a good starting point, but use your own preference to determine final amounts.

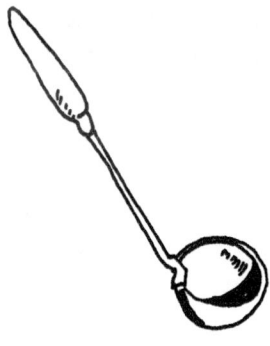

179

METTWURST AND BEANS

1 Pound Dried Great Northern Beans
2 x 2-Inch Piece Of Peppered Side Meat
1 Teaspoon Salt (Or To Taste)
4 Mettwurst Sausages
1 Can Chili Without Beans

Pick over dried beans to remove any gravel and bad beans. Wash the beans thoroughly, twice, and drain. Cover them with cold water, add seasoning meat scored but not cut through, cover and bring to a boil then reduce the heat to medium-low. Continue to cook covered until tender (about three hours). Stir occasionally and add water as necessary. After two hours, add the whole sausages to the beans. When the cooking time is almost done, add one teaspoon salt. To serve, place the sausages on a plate and slice crossways but not cutting all the way through, into bite-sized pieces. Spoon the white beans over the sausages and top with heated chili. Serve with cole slaw, pumpernickel bread, horseradish, sliced onions and pickle relish.

You will find no better winter meal. My cousin A.T. first introduced me to mett and beans at a little place on the UT campus in about 1965. Called Brownies, it has long since closed; I think when Brownie himself passed away. The taste, however, of this fine, hearty German dish always brings to mind that small, dark, cozy restaurant.

"Juke box and a sawdust floor, something like I ain't never seen; and I was just going on sixteen, but by the help of my finagling Uncle I get snuck in . . ."

R. Miller

180

Corned Beef And Cabbage

1 Whole Corned
   Beef, Any Size
1 Can Beets,
   Drained
Small Piece Salt
   Pork
3 Parsnips, Peeled
   And Quartered
5-6 Carrots,
   Scraped And
   Quartered
2-3 Turnips, Peeled
   And Quartered
10 Small or 5
   Medium Onions,
   Peeled and
   Quartered
6 Medium
   Potatoes, Peeled
   And Quartered
1 Medium Head
   Cabbage, Cut
   Into Wedges

Wash the corned beef under running water to remove any surface brine. In a large stock pot cover the beef with boiling water and simmer about one hour per pound until tender enough to pierce easily with a fork. In the last two hours of cooking, add the salt pork. When done, remove the corned beef from the pot and to the stock add the parsnips, carrots, turnips, and onions and cook for 30 minutes. Now, add the potatoes and cook an additional fifteen minutes. At the end of this time, add the cabbage and drained beets and cook an additional ten minutes. Slice an appropriate amount of the corned beef thinly, add to the above boiled dinner and heat through. Serve on a large platter, surrounded by the vegetables.

1½ Pounds Pea Or Navy Beans
4 Large Yellow Onions,
   Chopped
1 Large Clove Garlic
1 Tablespoon Butter
6 Stems Parsley
¾ Teaspoon Thyme
1½ Large Bay Leaves
1 Carrot, Chopped
½ Lemon, Sliced
1 Pound Smoked Ham Hock
Salt
Freshly Ground Black Pepper

Put the beans in a large bowl and add water to cover 4-5 inches. Let the beans soak overnight. Drain the beans and run them under hot water until they appear slightly whitened. Put the beans in a large soup pot and cover with three quarts cold water. Sauté the onions and garlic lightly in a little butter and add to the beans. Tie the parsley, thyme, bay leaves, carrot and lemon in cheesecloth and add to the beans. Add the ham hock and cover and cook slowly for about 3 hours or until reduced by half, and the beans are tender.

Remove the flavorings in the cheesecloth bag and discard. Remove the ham hock and let it cool. Take out two cups of the cooked beans with just a little liquid. Puree and return to the pot with an additional two cups of fresh water. Cut the ham into bite-sized pieces and return to the soup. Season with freshly ground pepper and one tablespoon salt. Reheat slowly and serve with corn bread and butter. Yield: eight servings.

Beef-Vegetable Soup

1½ Pounds Round
   Steak
1 Beef Soup Bone,
   Split
6-8 Medium
   Potatoes, Peeled
1 Large Onion
3 Carrots, Sliced
2 Stalks Celery
1 Quart Water
1 Quart Canned
   Tomatoes
1½ Teaspoon Salt
½ Teaspoon Freshly
   Ground Pepper
1 Clove Garlic
1 Tablespoon Oil

Cut the beef into bite-sized pieces, add a little salt and pepper and the minced garlic clove and place in a heated stock pot with just about one tablespoon of oil. Brown this mixture, stirring frequently. This should take only about ten minutes. Add one quart water and cook covered for one hour over medium-low heat.

After the meat is tender, add the soup bone; potatoes, peeled and quartered; onions, scraped and sliced; carrots; chopped celery and canned tomatoes with their juice. Cover and cook at medium-low for about ½ hour. Add salt and pepper to taste and cook covered for an additional ½ hour, or until the potatoes are tender. Reduce the heat to very low and simmer covered until ready to serve.

Use any beef that is on sale. Use any additional vegetables that are available. If cabbage is used, however, add it during the last ½ hour of cooking. If possible, ask the butcher to cut the soup bone in half and add both halves to the pot. This exposes the bone marrow which will give the soup an excellent flavor.

183

GRITTED CORNBREAD

4 Ears Of Corn
½ Teaspoon Salt
¼ Teaspoon Baking Soda

Use freshly pulled ears of corn that is past its prime "juicy" state. When corn is not picked at its peak, the kernels begin to harden. Use a coarse grater and grate the ears, being careful not to get any of the cob into the container. Mix all the ingredients and pour into a small, shallow, greased baking dish. Bake at 375 degrees for an hour, or until the bread is firm and browned. Serve hot with butter.

This is probably as close as you will ever get to the cornbread our pioneer forefathers made. I can imagine this being made up and placed in a greased dutch oven on the hearth of an open fireplace, with hot coals heaped on the lid.

To get an authentic picture of life in that era, visit the Appalachian Museum in Norris, Tennessee, about 20 miles north of Knoxville on Interstate 75. After you visit there, drive another 10 miles north, take the Caryville exit, visit LaFollette and try out a pool-room chili dog.

Potato Soup

Potatoes are truly one of God's very wonderful gifts. They are not mentioned in the Bible, except, in my view, indirectly:

"You will have plenty to eat, until you are full, and you will praise the name of the Lord your God, who has worked wonders for you ..." Joel 2:26

3 Medium Potatoes
2 Onions
4 Stalks Celery
4 Tablespoons Butter
½ Teaspoon Salt
1 Small Bay Leaf
1 Cup Half & Half
Dash Worcestershire Sauce
½ Teaspoon Salt
¼ Teaspoon Paprika
1 Cup Cooked Ham, Diced (Optional)

Peel and quarter the potatoes and chop the onion and celery. Sauté the onions and celery in a saucepan in ½ (two tablespoons) the butter. When golden, add the potatoes and enough water to cover, then add the salt and whole bay leaf. Bring to a boil and then reduce the heat and cook until the potatoes are tender. Remove the bay leaf. Put everything through a ricer, return to the pot, beat in the rest of the butter and add enough half-and-half to bring the soup to the desired consistency. Add Worcestershire sauce, paprika, and if needed, more salt to season. Add diced, cooked ham if desired and heat through.

185

CABBAGE AND BEAN SOUP

1½ Cup Dried White Beans
1 Smoked Ham Hock
   (12-16 Ounces)
5 Cloves Garlic, Crushed
1 Large Onion, Chopped
1 Teaspoon Rosemary
3 Carrots, Scraped and Sliced
4 Cups Cabbage, Shredded
   (About ½ Large
   Cabbage Head)
1 Teaspoon Salt (Add More
   To Taste If Necessary)
¾ Teaspoon Pepper,
   Freshly Ground

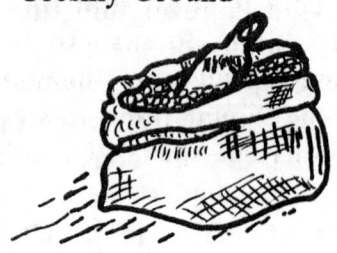

Rinse the beans and soak overnight, or for at least six hours. Drain and add ham, garlic, onion and eight cups of water. Bring the mixture to a boil, uncovered. Reduce the heat, cover, and simmer for about one hour. Add the remaining ingredients and simmer an additional hour. Makes four servings.

APPLE BUTTER

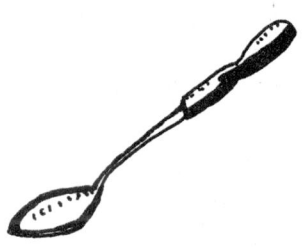

4 Quarts Apples, Peeled,
   Pared and Quartered
¼ Cup Vinegar
Powdered Cinnamon Or
   4 Cinnamon Sticks,
   3-4 Inches Long
Cloves
Sugar

Cover the apples with water and cook until they are soft. Rub through a sieve and then add half as much sugar as there is pulp. If, for instance you end up with four cups of pulp, then add two cups of sugar. However, if the apples are especially sour, add more sugar to taste. Return to the stove, and add vinegar, cinnamon and cloves. Simmer the mixture slowly, stirring constantly, until thick.

TENNESSEE HILL BISCUITS

2 Cups Self-Rising Flour
5 Tablespoons Shortening
1 Teaspoon Baking Powder
1 Teaspoon Sugar
¾ Cup Buttermilk

Mix all the dry ingredients and cut in the shortening until the mixture is crumbly. Add milk and mix lightly with hands until the dough holds together well. Turn onto a floured surface and roll to ¾-inch thick. Cut into biscuits and bake in a lightly greased pan at 400 degrees until golden brown. Makes 15-20 biscuits.

Carla's Grandma Cowan mixed up something she called "Larrup" for her family to eat with hot biscuits. She would cook together about ¾ cup of fresh berries and ⅓ cup flour until it was nice and thick and serve it hot to be used like preserves.

Some folks call these "Riz" biscuits, because, unlike regular biscuits they call for the addition of yeast, and must rise before baking. The action of the yeast gives them a lighter texture.
I believe the best biscuit maker I have known is Don Ed Dillingham. His early morning Men's Breakfasts with fried country ham was matchless; could be Glenda taught him something.

5 Cups All-Purpose Flour
1 Cup Shortening
1 Teaspoon Soda
1 Tablespoon Baking Powder
1 Tablespoon Sugar
1 Teaspoon Salt
1¾-2 Cups Buttermilk
¼ Cup Warm Water
1 Package Dry Yeast

Dissolve the yeast in the quarter cup of warm water. Set the yeast aside, and in another bowl blend the dry ingredients. Using a fork, thoroughly work in the shortening. Add the yeast mixture. Add the buttermilk and blend everything to make a soft dough. Start with 1¾ cups buttermilk, and add a bit more if needed to make the dough workable. Knead the dough only enough to cause it to hold together. On a floured surface, roll to about ½-inch thick. Cut biscuits with a floured biscuit cutter or the top of a glass or cup. Place them on a cookie sheet and bake in a 400 degree oven for about twenty minutes or until biscuits are golden brown.

BETH'S ANGEL BISCUITS

2½ Cups Sifted Self-Rising Flour
¼ Teaspoon Baking Soda
3 Tablespoons Sugar
1 Package Dry Yeast
1 Cup Buttermilk
⅓ Cup Shortening
½ Cup Melted Butter

Sift together the flour, soda, and sugar. Dissolve the yeast in warm buttermilk. Cut the shortening into the flour until the mixture is crumbly. Quickly stir the buttermilk-yeast mixture into the flour mixture. Turn the resulting dough onto a floured surface and knead just until it is smooth. Roll the dough to ¼-inch thick and cut it into biscuit shapes. Brush with melted butter and place biscuits one on top of another, making double biscuits. Set aside, covered with a cloth and let rise until double, about one hour. Bake in a 375 degree oven for twelve-fifteen minutes until golden brown.

The interesting thing about these biscuits is they are made in two layers. Anytime you make biscuits, handle the dough as little as possible after kneading. A heavy hand will make them tough.

These are called Angle Biscuits because they are so airy and light.

6-8 Parsnips
Broth from Pork Pot
Roast

Wash, peel and remove the ends of the parsnips. Remove a cooked pot roast from its broth. Quarter the parsnips and add to the broth. Cook the parsnips, covered at medium heat about ½-¾ hour, or until tender. Serve as a side dish with the pot roast.

BAKED SWEET POTATOES

3-4 Sweet Potatoes
(One For Each Person)
Cooking Oil
Butter

Wash and scrub the potatoes. Rub them with oil and place in a baking dish or pan. Do not wrap with foil. Bake about one hour in a 400 degree oven, or until a fork pierces the potatoes easily. Split and serve with butter.

191

Fried Pumpkin

2 Cups Cooked Pumpkin
  (Fresh Is Better Than Canned)
½ Cup Sugar
1 Teaspoon Salt (To Taste)
Pinch Of Cinnamon
Pinch Of Cloves
Pinch Of Nutmeg
Bacon Drippings or Oil

Heat oil or bacon drippings until hot, in a cast-iron skillet. Add the pumpkin, sugar salt and spices. Fry, stirring frequently until the liquid is gone. Serve with crisply fried thick style bacon and hot buttered biscuits.

Usually, when we think of pumpkins as food, pies are the first things that come to mind. The very first truly American cookbook, written by Amelia Simmons, though treats the pumpkin differently, as does this interesting recipe. In her book, the pumpkin was left whole and cleaned like a jack-o-lantern. It was then filled with maple syrup, milk and eggs, and baked, which turned it into a custard.

BISHOP'S PUDDING

1 Cup Chopped Pecans
1 Cup Chopped Dates
½ Pound Sugar
⅔ Cup Flour
2 Eggs, Beaten
1 Teaspoon Baking
    Powder

Beat the eggs, and mix with all the other ingredients as you would a cake. Bake in a shallow dish in a 350 degree oven until the cake is brown and the center is firm. Break into pieces while hot, and sprinkle with powdered sugar. Let cool and serve with whipped cream. Serves 8.

PERSIMMON PUDDING

2 Cups Persimmon Pulp
½ Stick Butter
1 Cup Sugar
1 Egg
1½ Cups Self-Rising
Flour
2 Cups Chopped Pecans

Pick the persimmons after the first frost; otherwise they will be unusable. Cream the butter and then continue beating and gradually add the sugar. Beat in the egg and then add the persimmon pulp alternately with the flour. Stir nuts into the mixture and bake in a nine-inch square greased pan in a 350 degree oven for about 50 minutes. Cool, cut into squares and serve with whipped cream.

The persimmon is an astringent plumlike fruit becoming sweet only when thoroughly ripe. There are both native and oriental varieties, the native tending to be puckery, even when ripe.

193

CREAMY PUMPKIN CUSTARD PIE

2 Cups Cooked Fresh Pumpkin
¾ Cup Sugar
3 Egg Yolks
½ Cup Milk
1 Cup Walnuts
½ Teaspoon Cloves
½ Teaspoon Salt
1 Teaspoon Cinnamon
1 Teaspoon Nutmeg
1 Teaspoon Vanilla Extract
1 Envelope Gelatin, Dissolved
    In ¼ Cup Water
1 Cup Whipping Cream,
    Whipped Very Stiff
1 Baked Pie Crust

Combine two cups of pumpkin and all the remaining ingredients except for the whipped cream and walnuts in the top of a double boiler and cook over boiling water until very thick. Cool the filling in the refrigerator. When completely cool, add walnuts; if it is still warm it will melt the whipped cream. Although not as good, you may substitute COOL WHIP for the whipped cream. Into a baked crust, add a layer of pie filling, cover with a layer of whipped cream, add another layer of pie filling, and garnish with whipped cream.

The pumpkin is really a type of squash, native to America. Although some grow to giant size, small garden varieties grow to 7-24 inches. The smaller ones are best for pies. The larger ones are grown for stock feed.

Mama's Pumpkin Pie

2 Cups Cooked
    Pumpkin
1 Cup Sugar
3 Eggs, Separated
1 Can Evaporated
    Milk (12 Ounce)
1 Teaspoon
    Cinnamon
½ Teaspoon Cloves
½ Teaspoon
    All Spice
½ Teaspoon
    Nutmeg
1 Teaspoon Vanilla
    Flavoring
2 Tablespoons
    Corn Starch
1 Baked Pie Shell
Meringue

Beat the egg yolks and reserve the whites for meringue. Place the pumpkin, sugar, yolks, evaporated milk, and spices into a double boiler. Note that the spices may be doubled if desired. Cook over boiling water until thick. A bit more corn starch may be added if necessary to thicken the filling. Spoon into a baked pie shell, top with meringue and place in a 350 degree oven until brown. For a different flavor, roll crushed pecans into the pie crust before you bake it.

APPLE DUMPLINGS

DUMPLING DOUGH

1½ Heaping Tsp. Baking Powder   ½ Tsp. Salt
1½ Tablespoons Shortening   1½ Cups Flour
          ½ Cup Milk, Or Enough To Moisten

APPLE MIXTURE

2 Cups Apples, Thinly Sliced
½ Cup Sugar
½ Teaspoon Cinnamon

LIQUID MIXTURE

1½ Cups Dark Brown Sugar
2 Cups Water
1½ Cups White Sugar

Cook the apples with a little water until soft. Mix the dumpling dough by sifting together the dry ingredients and then add enough milk to make the dough workable. Roll the dough out rather thin and then spread it with the cooked apples. Sprinkle ½ cup sugar and ½ teaspoon cinnamon over the apples to taste. If the apples are especially tart, use more sugar and cinnamon. Roll the dough and cooked apples like a jelly roll, then cut the roll into 4 large dumplings like cinnamon rolls. In a pan, mix together the brown sugar, water and 1½ cups white sugar and bring to a boil until well blended. Place the 4 dumplings into a baking dish, pour the liquid over and around the dumplings and bake in an ovenproof dish at 350° until brown.

In these days of instant potatoes and instant everything, exists the paradigm of all that is prepared slowly and excellently; Tennessee Country Ham. Others may argue that Virginia or Kentucky hams are just as good, but I have never been convinced. The flavor and aroma of an authentically baked country ham is beyond description. I saw a recipe once that called for the addition of Cola as a baste for a baked ham. I had to set down and regain my composure. Pat walked by and thought the dog had died, and began to comfort me before I was able to tell her different. If you use this recipe, invite me over.

BAKED COUNTRY HAM

1 Whole Country Ham
4 Tablespoons Cracker Crumbs
2 Tablespoons Brown Sugar
Black Pepper
Whole Cloves
1 Wineglass Cooking Sherry

Scrub, clean and remove fat, and then soak a ten-twelve pound Tennessee or Virginia Country-Cured Ham for twelve hours in a large container. Mama used to use a huge lard can. Drain and renew the water in the container. Next, boil, cooking very slowly for four-five hours, until tender. Cool the ham in its own liquid. When cold, remove the skin and make crisscross gashes in the ham with a sharp knife. Sprinkle on top of the ham four tablespoons of cracker dust, two tablespoons of brown sugar, and dust lightly with freshly ground black pepper. Stick the ham with whole cloves. Sprinkle lightly over this, a wineglass of sherry. Don't pour the wine all at one time, but drizzle it very gently so as not to wash off the sugar, etc. Bake in a 450 degree oven for 20-30 minutes until brown.

197

Refrigerator Rolls

¾ Cup Shortening
2 Eggs, Beaten
7½ Cups Shifted Flour
1 Cup Hot Scalded Milk, Or 1
    Cup Boiling Water
¾ Cup Sugar
2 Teaspoons Salt
2 Envelopes Yeast
1 Cup Cold Water
½ Cup Lukewarm Water

Combine the shortening and boiling water (or hot scalded milk) and stir until the shortening is melted. Combine the beaten eggs, sugar and salt, and into this beat the cold water. Add two envelopes of yeast dissolved in lukewarm water. Make sure the water for the yeast is not too hot, as it will cause the dough not to rise. Add the flour, two cups at a time, until your dough is the correct consistency. Cover and chill overnight in the refrigerator. The next day, roll the dough to a little over ¼-inch thick, cut them into 2½-inch circles, and fold the circles over to a semi-circle to make individual rolls. Cover with a cloth and let them rise for about two hours in a warm place, brush each one with butter and then bake in a lightly greased pan at 375° for 20-25 minutes until lightly browned. This will make about 36 rolls, and the recipe may be halved for fewer rolls.

CHOCOLATE FUDGE

5 Cups Sugar
2 Sticks Butter
  (Not Margarine)
1 Large or 2 Small
  Cans Evaporated
  Milk (12 Ounces
  Total)
1 Package
  Semi-Sweet
  Chocolate Mini-
  Morsels
  (12 Ounces)
1 Jar Marshmallow
  Creme (14
  Ounces)
1 Cup English
  Walnuts, Broken
  Into Small
  Pieces
2 Teaspoons
  Vanilla Extract

Mix the sugar, butter and evaporated milk. Heat over medium heat in a large heavy pan until it comes to a rolling boil and then continue cooking for about ten minutes, stirring constantly. Remove the pan from the heat, add chocolate chips, marshmallow creme, and vanilla. Beat by hand with a large spoon until the mixture thickens and turns from glossy to dull. If it does not thicken in 20-30 minutes of beating, add two-three tablespoons of powdered sugar a little at-a-time. Add nuts, mix thoroughly and spread to about ¾-1-inch thick in a buttered pan that is about 11 x 14 x 1-inches deep. Allow to cool, covered at room temperature overnight and then cut into squares. Store in an airtight container, separated by waxed paper.

This is a smooth, creamy fudge, and never becomes grainy. It takes a lot of hand beating, and I believe hand beating is somehow better than using an electric mixer. Mama makes it every Christmas, and we pass the bowl around as we beat it. One person works until their arm becomes tired, and then it is given to someone else.

HOLIDAY DIVINITY

2¾ Cups Sugar
¾ Cups Water
¾ Cups White Syrup
2 Egg Whites
1 Teaspoon Vanilla
1 Cup Chopped Red Candied
   Cherries
½ Cup Chopped Pecans

With an electric mixer, beat the egg whites until they are stiff. Combine the sugar, water and syrup and cook over low heat in a heavy saucepan to the hard ball stage, 160°. Pour this cooked blend slowly in a thin stream over the two beaten egg whites as you continue beating at high speed as the syrup mixture is added. Continue until the divinity begins to hold its shape; this should take about four minutes. If the mixture does not thicken properly, add a little powdered sugar. Add vanilla, chopped candied cherries (not maraschino) and chopped nuts. Blend and drop by rounded teaspoons into a buttered pan or drop by teaspoons onto waxed paper. Let the candy cool and store uneaten candy in air-tight container. This will make about 60 pieces of divinity.

One of my childhood memories of Christmas is this divinity, along with chocolate fudge squares, displayed on a JEWEL TEA serving tray.

JEWEL TEA dinnerware was sold by the JEWEL TEA COMPANY that came around to customers houses about once a month. The housewife could buy dishes, or they were available as free premiums with certain purchases.

They sold everything from brassieres to spices.

200

PEANUT BUTTER ROLL

2 Cups Granulated
Sugar
¼ Cup Water
2 Egg Whites
1½ Teaspoon
Vanilla
Flavoring
1-1½ Cups
Powdered
(Confectioner's)
Sugar
1 Jar Creamy
Peanut Butter,
Softened
(16 Ounce)

Soften the peanut butter by placing the container in a pan of warm water. In a heavy saucepan, combine two cups of granulated sugar and ¼ cup water and cook over medium heat to the hard crack stage (300°-310°). Using a large bowl and an electric mixer, beat the egg whites until they form stiff peaks and then add the syrup you prepared from the sugar-water mixture, in a slow stream. Add the vanilla, beating on high. When the mixture is stiff, gradually add powdered sugar a little at-a-time until it is just thick enough to handle. Cover a large piece of waxed paper with powdered sugar almost ½-inch thick. Work the resulting confection in the powdered sugar until it absorbs the sugar and is no longer sticky. This is a messy procedure, but you really *do* need that much powdered sugar on the waxed paper. Using your hands, form a rectangle about ½-inch thick, patting it into shape. With a wide knife or similar tool, spread a ¼-inch layer of softened peanut butter over the top of the confection. Using two table knives, and working away from yourself, gently roll the entire doohickey into a long cylinder. This is a slow process, and you will think you need another hand, but thinking gentle thoughts, coax it into shape. Slice the roll crossways and place the resulting pinwheel-like circles into a cake tin in single layers with waxed paper between each layer. Cover tightly as the candy dries out quickly when uncovered.

201

STACK CAKE

1½ Cups Sugar	2 Cups Flour
3 Tablespoons Shortening	½ Teaspoon Cloves
2 Eggs, Beaten	½ Teaspoon Cinnamon
½ Teaspoon Soda	½ Teaspoon Nutmeg
2 Tsp. Baking Powder	1½ Teaspoon Vanilla
3 Cups Cooked Apples	

Beat all the ingredients together, except for the dry spices and apples, until well blended. In six, eight-inch greased and floured pans, bake six layers, adding about ¼-inch of the batter to each pan. Mama says she uses about ½ cup of batter per pan. Pour the batter into the middle of the pan and then use the bottom of a tablespoon and spread to the edges. It won't seem very thick, but bakes into a crisp cookie-like layer. Not many folks have six pans, so you will probably need to bake two or three at a time. Bake in a 350° oven for about 7-10 minutes until brown.

Add cinnamon, cloves and nutmeg to the three cups of cooked apples to suit your personal taste. Use more spices if you prefer. When the layers have cooled, carefully remove them from their pans and spread about ½ cup of the apple mixture on the bottom layer, add the next layer, etc. alternating apples and cake until all the cake layers and apples are used. Do not spread apples on top of the cake. Cover tightly and let the stack cake set overnight before serving.

Mama says dried apples are best, for that's what her mother (my Granny Bess) used when she was a girl. The apples would be picked and dried during the summer or fall, dried in the sun, and put away until they were needed. You can find dried apples in the grocery, and if you use commercially dried fruit, it is best to cook and flavor them the night before you assemble your stack cake.

Cooked fresh apples are good too. Winesap apples are a good choice if you want to use fresh apples, and you can also use canned apples, although they must be cooked some on the stove top until they have the pudding-like consistency needed for spreading.

To dry your own apples, improvise trays that look like old-fashioned window screens—but don't actually *use* old screens as the metal in them will contaminate the fruit. Make a simple rectangular frame and staple or nail non-metallic screening material to it. Support the frame on bricks and place it on any hot outdoor surface such as a heat reflecting driveway or rooftop. Next, put the apples on the frame and place blocks of wood at each corner. Over this, drape cheesecloth and weight it down around the edges with more bricks too keep it from blowing off. Put the apples out on sunny summer or early fall days after the dew has dried and bring them back in at dusk, or cover them with plastic. If you have a cat, encourage her to hang around to discourage birds.

The apples will be ready when about 85-90 percent of the moisture has been removed. This will ensure that the growth of spoiling bacteria has been eliminated. To help retain the flavor, as you peel and slice the apples, dip the pieces in pure lemon juice. A cup of lemon juice will process about five quarts of cut fruit. The best temperature for drying is 95-140° (the U.S. Department of Agriculture recommends 140 degrees) so you must have a rather hot day and have the fruit on a surface that becomes hotter than the surrounding air temperature.

To be absolutely safe, after the fruit has dried outside sufficiently, preheat your oven to 175°, spread the apples about an inch deep on cookie trays and place them in the oven for 10-15 minutes. This will insure that no insect eggs or spoilage microorganisms remain.

Place the dried fruit in clean, sterilized glass jars. Leave the jars open for about five days and stir daily. Finally, seal the jars by screwing on lids and place them in a cool dark place. The fruit may sweat if stored in an area warmer than about 60 degrees.

2¼ Cups Sifted Cake Flour
3 Teaspoons Baking Powder
¼ Teaspoon Soda
½ Teaspoon Salt
1 Teaspoon Cinnamon
1 Teaspoon Ginger
½ Cup Granulated Sugar
½ Cup Butter
1 Cup Brown Sugar (Packed)
¾ Cup Canned Pumpkin
½ Cup Buttermilk, halved
1 Egg (Yolks and White)
2 Eggs Yolks (Yolks Only)

Measure the sifted flour, add baking powder, soda, salt, spices and white sugar. Mix well. Place the butter into a mixing bowl and stir just enough to soften. To the butter add the dry ingredients, brown sugar, pumpkin and ¼ cup of the buttermilk. Blend with a spoon and then beat at low speed for 2 minutes, or 300 strokes by hand. Add the 1 egg plus 2 yolks and the remaining ¼ cup buttermilk. Beat 1 minute longer at low speed or 150 strokes by hand. Line the bottoms of 2, eight-inch layer pans with waxed paper. Pour the batter into the pans and bake at 350° for about 30 minutes. Frost with Seven Minute Icing,

What about cake mixes? Admittedly, they save time, usually a considerable amount, but that seems to me to be their only advantage. It is a fact that they do not save money, if you consider that when you purchase the ingredients for a particular cake, you have enough left over to make several more. If you really want to impress your friends with your cooking ability, pick out a few good cakes and perfect your methods for making them. You will find that as you repeat each recipe you will be doing it much quicker and easier, and will end up with an infinitely superior product.

GEORGIA PECAN PIE

If you substitute a teaspoon of rum flavoring, or 3 teaspoons bourbon for the vanilla, you will have a pie of an entirely different nature.

3 Whole Eggs
2 Tablespoons Melted Butter
2 Tablespoons Flour
¼ Teaspoon Vanilla
⅛ Teaspoon Salt
½ Cup Brown Sugar
1½ Cups White Corn Syrup
1½ Cups Broken Pecan Halves
1 Unbaked 8-inch Pie Shell

Beat the eggs, and blend in melted butter, flour, vanilla, salt, sugar and syrup. Sprinkle nuts over the bottom of an unbaked pastry shell. Gently pour the syrup mixture over the nuts and bake in a preheated 425 degree oven for ten minutes. Reduce the heat to 325 degrees and bake about 40 minutes more.

MAMA'S PECAN PIE

4 Eggs
1 Cup Granulated Sugar
1 Cup White Syrup
1½ teaspoon Vanilla
1 Cup Pecan Halves
9-Inch Unbaked Pie Shell

Beat the eggs well and to them add sugar, syrup, vanilla and the pecan halves. Mix well and pour into an unbaked pie shell. Bake in a 375 degree oven until a knife comes out clean, about 35-40 minutes.

I like this pecan pie recipe because it is not overly sweet. Many I have eaten were so rich one could only enjoy a very small portion.

Be sure your oven is not too hot, for this pie must bake slowly. Otherwise, the crust will burn before the pie is done.

Mama says to use a silver knife to test doneness.

PECAN POUND CAKE

This is a wonderful Christmas holiday cake to compliment your traditional fruit-cake.

In the fall, the ground is covered with pecans at the courthouse in Rogersville, just about two doors down from the **HALE SPRINGS INN**.

1 Pound Butter
2 Cups Sugar
6 Eggs, Well Beaten
1 Tablespoon Lemon Extract
4 Cups All-Purpose Flour, Sifted
1½ Teaspoons Baking Powder
4 Cups Pecan Halves
2 Cups White Raisins

Preheat oven to 300 degrees. Grease and flour a 9¾-inch tube pan. In a large bowl blend the butter and sugar, beating until the mixture is light and fluffy. Gradually add the eggs and lemon extract and continue to beat until well blended. In a separate bowl, sift flour and baking powder together three times; add the pecans and raisins to the flour. Gradually add the flour mixture to the creamed butter and sugar and blend thoroughly. Pour this into the tube pan and bake 1½-2 hours. Cool for fifteen minutes before removing from the pan and then allow the cake to cool completely.

207

ORANGE FLAN

¾ Cup Sugar
3 Tablespoons Boiling Water
6 Eggs
1 Can Sweetened Condensed
   Milk
1 Can Evaporated Milk
   (12 Ounce)
¼ Cup Orange Juice
2 Tablespoons Orange Peel,
   Finely Grated
1 Teaspoon Vanilla Extract

Preheat the oven to 325 degrees. Spread the sugar evenly over the bottom of an iron skillet and cook over medium heat, stirring constantly, until the sugar melts and turns a light caramel color. Add the three tablespoons of boiling water and stir until the sugar is dissolved. Pour this into a ten-inch glass deep dish piepan, tilting the plate to evenly distribute the caramelized sugar mixture. Set the plate aside. In a medium bowl combine the remaining ingredients and beat at medium speed for two minutes or until the mixture is well blended. Pour this mixture over the sugar in the piepan. Place the piepan into a large pan and set in the oven and add one inch of hot water. Bake at 325 degrees for 40-45 minutes or until the Flan is almost set and a knife inserted in the center comes out clean. Cool completely in the refrigerator. Gently loosen the sides with a table knife, place a serving plate on top of the piepan and invert to remove and serve.

This is not a Souther Appalachian dish, but has its origins in Cuba. Nevertheless it is delicious, proving that Tennessee hill folks have no monopoly on good ethnic food.

Mark's Mama, Kathy Hamilton, makes this every Thanksgiving.

3 Eggs, Separated
3 Tablespoons Sugar
¾ Cup Cream, Half & Half Or Milk
3 Tablespoons Rum Flavoring
Dash Of Salt

Beat the egg yolks until they are a light color and then slowly beat in sugar, cream, flavoring and salt. In a separate bowl, whip the egg whites until they become stiff and then fold them lightly into the other ingredients. This recipe makes about three servings. Garnish the nog generously with freshly ground nutmeg.

Note that this recipe calls for uncooked eggs. The use of unpasteurized, uncooked eggs has recently been reported to have the potential to cause illness.

BOILED CUSTARD

2 Cups Scalded Milk
6 Egg Yolks
¼ Cup sugar
⅛ Teaspoon salt
½ Teaspoon Vanilla

Beat the eggs with a fork and then add the sugar and salt. Add scalded milk gradually, stirring constantly. Place in the top of a double boiler and cook over hot but not boiling water, stirring constantly. Continue cooking until the custard coats a spoon, about seven minutes. This will curdle if over-cooked. If this happens, beat with an electric mixer to restore.

2 Pounds Boneless Beef (Sirloin or Tenderloin)
½ Cup Flour
½ Teaspoon Accent
1 Teaspoon Salt
⅛ Teaspoon Pepper, Freshly Ground
⅓ Cup Butter
½ Cup Onion, Finely Chopped
2 Cups Canned Beef Broth
3 Tablespoons Butter
½ Pound Fresh Mushrooms, Sliced
1 Cup Commercial Sour Cream
3 Tablespoons Tomato Paste
1 Teaspoon Worcestershire Sauce

Cut the beef into ¼-inch slices and then into strips one-two inches long. Pound them until thin. Mix the flour, Accent, salt and pepper; dip the meat into this mixture to coat the pieces. Heat ⅓ cup butter in a large skillet; add the onion and sauté for about two minutes. Add the beef, and sauté quickly in the onion-butter mixture until brown, about 5 minutes. Add the beef broth and cover and simmer for 20-25 minutes, or until the meat is fork tender. While the meat is cooking, melt 3 tablespoons butter in a small skillet and cook the mushrooms for about 5 minutes, or until lightly browned.

When the meat has cooked, combine the sour cream, tomato paste and Worcestershire sauce; add ½ cup of the stock from the meat to this mixture, and stir until blended. Gradually pour this back into the skillet with the meat-onion mixture and combine well. Add the browned mushrooms and heat, but do not boil. Serve over rice. This dish freezes well. Yield: six servings.

Spaghetti Sauce

2 Stalks Celery
1 Medium Green Pepper
1 Large Onion
1 Pound Hamburger
½-¾ Pound Bulk Italian Sausage
6 Italian Sausage Links
1 Large Container Canned Or ½ Pound Fresh Mushrooms
4 Large Cans Tomato Sauce
1 Can Tomato Paste (12 Ounce)
5 Bay Leaves, Whole
2½ Teaspoons Oregano
¾ Teaspoon Chili Powder
1½ Teaspoon Parsley Flakes
2 Teaspoon Garlic Salt
2 Teaspoons Honey
1 Bottle Sharps Non-Alcoholic Beer (12 Ounce)

Chop the onions, celery and pepper and sauté them in butter until tender. Remove the mixture and use the same skillet to brown the hamburger, bulk sausage and sausage links along with the mushrooms. Drain the meat-mushroom mixture. In a large pot, combine all the spices, tomato paste and tomato sauce and bring them to a boil over medium heat. Add the onion-pepper mixture, meat-mushroom and sausage link mixture. Cook covered at low heat for one hour. Taste and adjust the spices or salt if needed. Add a portion of the beer to bring the mixture to the correct thickness. Cook covered for an additional five hours on low heat. Check the thickness again before the last hour and adjust with the remaining beer if needed. If no more beer is needed, give it to the dog. Simmer the last hour with the pot uncovered.

Cook the spaghetti as the package directions indicate, using the **lower** figure for the cooking time. Pasta needs to be al dentes; just a bit on the chewy side. Do not overcook.

Serve your Spaghetti Sauce over the cooked pasta with generous amounts of grated Parmesan cheese and buttered garlic bread.

HOT TAMALE PIE

6 Cups Boiling Water
2 Cups Corn Meal
2 Tablespoons Cooking Oil
1 Pound Hamburger
1 Onion, Chopped
½ Green Pepper, Chopped
2 Cups Canned Tomatoes
Salt
Pepper

Sift the cornmeal slowly into rapidly boiling water, stirring constantly. Cook for fifteen minutes, and then set aside. Brown the hamburger, onion and green pepper in hot oil. Add the canned tomatoes to the meat, season to taste, and simmer for ten minutes. Fill a well-oiled baking dish with alternate layers of the corn meal mush and the meat mixture. Bake in a 400° oven for about twenty minutes. Serve hot.

Although not a dish that originated in the Southern Appalachians, this reminds me of the "full house" I used to buy at a little stand-up restaurant on Gay Street in Knoxville.

A "full house" is a bowl of chili topped with a hot tamale.

If you have trouble finding good veal for Wiener Schnitzel, ask at a specialty meat market. They will sometimes carry the more expensive and difficult to find cuts that the large super markets find hard to move. In Morristown, ask Sam Moore at SAM'S MEAT CLEAVER on West Andrew Johnson Highway.

WIENER SCHNITZEL

1½ Pounds Veal Cutlet
1-2 Cups Cracker
  Or Commercial Bread Crumbs
¾ Cup Butter

Pound the veal to ¼-inch thick. Coat the meat with fine cracker crumbs and let stand for at least fifteen minutes. In a large, heavy skillet, melt the butter and sauté the veal exactly two minutes on each side. Turn the third time and continue to cook until done, but not more than ten minutes more. Top with a fried egg to serve, if you are really interested in deliciously increasing your cholesterol intake.

213

Paprika Veal

Veal Steaks, Pounded ½-Inch
  Thick
1 Cup Flour
1 Teaspoon Salt
½ Teaspoon Pepper
¼ Cup Cooking Oil
2 Large Onions, Sliced
1-2 Tablespoons Paprika
½ Cup Sour Cream

Place flour, salt and pepper into a paper bag. Add the pounded veal steaks and shake vigorously to coat. Add oil to a cast-iron skillet and heat to medium. Add paprika to the hot oil until the oil turns red, then add the two sliced onions. Sauté the onions, add meat, and brown on both sides. To this mixture, gradually add ½ cup sour cream thinned with a little milk. Add salt to taste, cover pan, reduce heat and cook slowly for ½ hour.

Paprika Veal is similar to stroganoff, but more spicy. Although not necessarily a southern dish, it is none-the-less ethnic, evolving from our Hungarian ancestors.

Do not purchase cheap paprika. It has very little flavor and is useful only for color as a garnish.

FINALLY

Finally, all of you, live in harmony with one another; be sympathetic, love as brothers, be compassionate and humble. 1 Peter 3:8

HE SAT ON THE COUCH, the dog sleeping by his side, its head on his leg. Nearby, his daughter pored over an English Literature textbook reading of the tragedy of the deaths of Romeo and Juliet. His wife moved around in the kitchen, the sizzle and fragrance of dinner drifting into the den. Natalie Cole's voice came softly from the CD player's speakers, as she sang her father's song *Mona Lisa*.

How does one end a book? How does one finish any project? What should be the thing that puts, simply and honestly, the period at the end of the final sentence?

He stood, causing the sleeping dog to grunt its dissatisfaction. It moved to the end of the couch, pushed its nose behind a cushion, sighed and returned to its nap.

The man walked to the bookcase and looked for a minute. "Beth, have you seen my Bible? I thought it was here in the bookcase."

"Ummm? Oh, you had it in the living room, Daddy;

over beside the rocker."

"Thanks." He retrieved the Bible and sat down again beside the dog. It raised its head, looked at him for a moment in disgust and went back to sleep.

He read for a few minutes, flipping through the pages. He raised his voice so he could be heard in the kitchen. "Pat, I'm looking for a verse that talks about using prayer in every situation. It has the word *supplication* in it. You remember where it is?"

She thought for a second. "No, I do know the one you mean, but I can't remember the reference. Look in the *Strong's Concordance.*"

"Can't find it. You'd think a book that big couldn't be lost."

He flipped some more. Pat came to the door. "Call your Mama. She probably knows where it is."

Absorbed in Shakespeare, the girl had missed all this. "Mom, when's supper?"

"Just about ten minutes, as soon as the bread is done. Come help me set the table."

He was talking to his mother on the phone. "Okay. Thanks, I'll look there. See you in the morning."

"Do not be anxious about anything, but in everything, by prayer and petition, with thanksgiving, present your requests to God. And the peace of God, which transcends all understanding, will guard your hearts and your minds in Christ Jesus. Finally, brothers, whatever is true, whatever is noble, whatever is right, whatever is pure, whatever is lovely, whatever is admirable—if anything is excellent or praiseworthy—think about such things." Philippians 4:6-8

So, there is the answer, and I will end as I started, with a prayer. It is for both you, the reader, and for me.

Father, thank you for your gift of life, and for the provision you have made to sustain it. You give us food, drink and breath; but equally important, you have given us each other. Create in us, through Your Spirit, the consuming desire to cultivate and cherish those relationships; for of everything we have in this life, our character, born of the love we have for each other and for you is all we will bring, finally, into your presence.

Recipe Index

220

Notes

ORDER FORM

Thank you for purchasing this book. If you would like to buy more copies, fill out and remove this page and mail to the address below.

YES! Please send _____ copies of *God's Grace, Chili Dogs & Supper At Mama's.*

_____ copies x $12.95 each   _____

Tennessee addresses add $1.10
        per book Sales Tax   _____

Add $2.00 per book shipping
        (Maximum amount $5.00)   _____

TOTAL ENCLOSED $ _____

Ship To

Name_____

Address_____

City_____State___Zip_____

Allow 2 Weeks For Delivery

Mail To:

PARNASSUS PUBLISHING;
P.O. Box 14202
Morristown, TN 37814

Notes